WHAT HAVE THE ROMANS EVER DONE FOR US?

COLIN C. MURPHY

CYGNIA
PUBLISHING

FIND OUT MORE...

For a free copy of 'The Lost Voices - Prelude',
which is the electrifying introduction to
Colin C. Murphy's ancient Pompeian trilogy and
to discover more about his other books, along with
news of forthcoming projects, visit his website,
which you'll find at the end of
What Have The Romans Ever Done For Us?

To the memory of the innumerable Roman engineers, artists, sculptors, astronomers, architects and authors whose names have been lost but whose works still shine brightly in our modern world.

INTRODUCTION

What Have The Roman Ever Done For Us?

*30 ways in which the ancient Romans
influence our lives today.*

The Roman State, either as a Republic or an Empire, existed for 1,000 years and encompassed a vast area spanning Europe, the Middle East and Africa. Their influence was so enormous that even though the Roman Empire ended 1,600 years ago, we can still feel their presence in our everyday lives, although most of the time we aren't usually aware of the fact. Everything from our architecture to our calendar, from our infrastructure to our spoken and written language, from our legal systems to many of the traditions we take for granted - all can trace their roots back through the centuries to the days of Augustus and Caesar.

So let's travel back to the time of the ancients, and explore how we can still sense their spirits in our modern world.

1
ADVERTISING

You'd probably imagine that the modern concepts of PR and marketing were a relatively new phenomenon, perhaps stretching back to the days of the town crier, but we have the ancient Romans to thank for introducing the world to the advert, something so irritatingly ubiquitous nowadays that we should probably curse them for their innovation.

Of course the ancient world didn't have the vast banquet of media options that we face today. There were no newspapers, television, radio or search engine marketing & optimisation, (whatever that is). There weren't even leaflets or junk mail. But there was still a multiplicity of ways the Roman businessman or businesswoman could promote their wares, or themselves, for that matter. (Although women had less rights than men and could not vote, they did have the right to own and operate private businesses, and there is evidence that many of them did so very successfully.)

One of these was the simple sponsorship of news broadcasts. It was common practice in towns all over the Roman Republic or Empire to send a man to the forum to inform his fellow citizens about news from far away places, such as the glorious defeat of an enemy army in North Africa or the completion of a new road in Greece. In towns all over Italy, news would regularly be announced of developments in Rome (and many Roman citizens, even Italians had never even visited their capital city). So the *'praeco'* or 'shouter' would stand in an elevated position and project his voice across the forum for all to hear, and when finished with the news, he would often append his performance by informing the *vulgus* (or common people) that 'the finest bread in town will be found in the bakery of Marcus Fabius' or that 'the Inn of Fulvio offers patrons private bathing to rival that of Caracalla's Baths in Rome'. These weren't officially sponsored, of course, but no doubt the *praeco* had been slipped a handful of denarii beforehand to deliver the message.

Wine advert with prices in the Bottega ad Cucumas,
(Shop of Cucumas) in Herculaneum.
(Photo by Jebulon)

ONE PLACE the Romans could compete with modern marketing

was on the walls of a town, nowadays adorned with massive posters, back then with something less brash, but no less effective. Business owners often hired a skilled sign-writer to go to one of the streets that had a large footfall and paint a sign promoting his or her product. There is ample evidence of this in Pompeii and its neighbouring town, Herculaneum, where multiple adverts were revealed when the ash was dusted painstakingly away. One such example was provided by the wealthy Pompeian property tycoon and politician Gnaeus Alleius Maius, who had his slave Primus advertise a block of apartments:

The city block of the Arrii Pollii in the possession of Gnaeus Alleius Nigidius Maius is available to rent from July 1st. There are shops on the first floor, upper stories, high-class rooms and a house. A person interested in renting this property should contact Primus, the slave of Gnaeus Alleius Nigidius Maius.

Painting slogans on walls was beloved of politicians advertising themselves (see also Political Campaigning). Prostitutes too availed of the Pompeians' love of defacing their walls and in another example from just outside the Marine Gate in Pompeii, a girl called Attice advertises her wares:

Si quis hic sederit, legat hoc ante omnia.
Si qui futuere voluit Atticen, quaerat assibus IV.

If anyone sits here, let him read this first of all:
if anyone wants a fuck, he should look for Attice:
I cost 4 sesterces.

Another means of advertising was on the products themselves – and for one man in particular it proved very successful.

(See also Variety – Trademarks.) Umbricius Scaurus was a manufacturer of *garum* (a sauce made from rotting mackerel!) that was beloved of Romans. Many of the amphorae from his workshop were adorned with ads promoting his product:

*Scaurus' finest mackerel sauce from
Scaurus' workshop,
made by Martial, imperial freedman.*

Scaurus cleverly also employed more permanent ads in the form of murals and mosaics to advertise his product, and it proved so successful that he owned about forty per cent of the business in Campania, and his sauce was exported to Rome and even France.

When it came to public relations and self-publicity, the Romans were masters. Wealthy Romans who wished to be loved by the masses or remembered long after they'd kicked the bucket, had many options. One of the most common was the sponsorship of games, gladiatorial contests or theatre. Entry into these events was generally free, the only price the spectators had to pay was having to listen to a *praeco* bellowing out the wonderful attributes of the games' sponsor, his kindness and generosity, his loyalty to Rome, his mercifulness etc. Here's an example from ancient Pompeii of a 'coming soon' advert inscribed on a wall:

*For the well-being of Nero Claudius Caesar Augustus Germanicus, at Pompeii,
there will be a hunt, athletics, and sprinklings by Tiberius Claudius Verus on 25–26 February.
Good fortune to Claudius Verus.*

Another method of lauding oneself widely was the use of

currency. Emperors regularly had coins minted bearing their likeness, often accompanied by inscriptions informing the world of his military victories and how generally wonderful a fellow he was. The Emperor could then relax in the knowledge that every time someone went to buy a loaf of bread or pay a prostitute for sex, they'd always be reminded of his divine presence looking after them.

But from the glories of the Emperor, let's finish with a much more prosaic - and cheaper - form of advertising: graffiti. There are lots of examples of tradesmen using graffiti across the Roman world, particularly in Pompeii. Textile makers lauded the quality of their linen, moneylenders their rates, engravers their skills. And then there was this chap, extolling the food and bathing facilities of the Suburban Baths, along with an extra service the facility provided:

Apelles the waiter dined most pleasantly here with Dexter the slave of the emperor, and they had a fuck at the same time.

They certainly made a meal of their visit.

2

AGRICULTURE

It's not surprising that the Romans were great innovators when it came to working the land – they really had no choice. At its peak the population of the capital was about one million, making it the most populated city on earth. That's a lot of hungry mouths to feed. Even in 100 BC the population numbered almost half a million, which was gargantuan for the era. Add to that, Rome had to provide its moving armies with a constant supply of food and materials, all of which meant that the lone subsistence farmer was soon put out to seed. The huge demands required a new way of approaching agriculture to make it more efficient and productive. As a result, the Romans developed techniques that we're still using today.

As Rome expanded during the early centuries of its existence, the small farmer eventually became all but extinct, his land swallowed whole by the development of *latifundia* – vast farming estates owned and controlled by wealthy men, who had often been granted the land by the state in return for military service. These lands were largely worked by slave labour, which seriously reduced the overheads for the owner.

But the slaves weren't the only reason farming became

highly profitable. It was during this period that the Romans realised that the concept of crop rotation could greatly improve productivity. The scale of the farms also meant that they could rotate various crops around multiple fields without growing the same one in the same field for as much as four or five years, greatly improving yields. Crop rotation is still employed on farms today to prevent the de-nutrifying of soil.

A fresco in the Dominus Julius in Carthage. The image portrays daily life on a farming estate, with the workers and slaves supplying the owner's household with the lavish bounty of the earth. (Photo by O. Mustafin. Bardo National Museum, Tunis)

It didn't stop there. The Romans employed their extensive network of aqueducts to irrigate the land, and also used the water to drive mills, which ground wheat into flour without having to transport it to some faraway mill driven by mules or oxen. In one case at Barbegai, near Arles in France, the Romans built a series of sixteen mills in two columns on a slope, fed by the nearby aqueduct. The resulting capacity of the mill was almost five tons of flour per day, which is comparable to the output of a medium-sized modern-day factory. This has been referred to as 'the greatest known concentration of mechanical power in the ancient world', although it was by no means unique in the empire, and its development inspired the building of water-powered mills for farming across the millennium to follow.

The Romans also perfected techniques for pruning, seed selection (removing poor strains), grafting and fertilising, many of which are still used in the modern era.

Given their agricultural innovations, its little wonder that Rome could itself grow with such vitality as the centuries advanced.

3
ALPHABET

You're reading it this instant – perhaps the single most ubiquitous and visible legacy of ancient Rome in the modern world. The Latin alphabet. It's all around us, in every country in the western world. On road signs, in books, in newspapers and on the back of the microwavable chicken curry you bought in the local convenience store.

Originally developed by the Etruscans, the race from north of Rome (who would be eventually subsumed into the Roman Republic), the Romans adopted their form of writing and subsequently adapted it to their needs and added to it by, for example, borrowing Y and Z from the Greek alphabet to fit their word sounds. They also introduced the technique of writing it from left to right. Having settled on the capital letters, by the third century they had also developed what became Roman cursive script, better known to you and I as lower case letters, which was used for more informal writing i.e. 'a, b, c, d...'

A 2,000-year old inscription on the Tomb of Mamia in Pompeii, using the very same alphabet we use today. (Photo by Colin C. Murphy)

BY THE FIFTH century AD the alphabet had spread to the entire Roman Empire, and was being used from the borders of Scotland to what is now the eastern border of Iraq. Then along came Christianity, who also adopted Latin as their form of writing. The expansion of the religion into Northern Europe, parts of Africa and the Americas saw the Roman alphabet's use take on global proportions. And today it is the most used form of writing on the planet.

It is sobering to walk through the forum in Rome or around any ancient Roman site and see words carved into stone using the very same ABC's that we would learn as children two thousand years later. It's a legacy that's almost too good for words.

4

AQUEDUCTS

As with agriculture, the expansion of Rome also demanded a regular supply of fresh water to drink primarily, and also to bring their countless fountains to life, to flush out their toilets, and in which to bathe, which the Romans did at every possible opportunity. (See also Sanitation.) Getting water to mines, mills, farms and even gardens (which supplied a not insubstantial amount of a town's food supply) was also key to keep the economy running and the countless bellies full.

Building an aqueduct is no easy thing and required feats of engineering that were comparable to the construction of the pyramids, and in many ways outshone even those in technical brilliance.

The Aqua Traiana, for example, named after the Emperor Trajan who commissioned it, channelled water from Lake Bracciano, over a distance of forty kilometres to the heart of Rome. This was a mere baby, as others like that in Carthage stretched for ninety kilometres, and the Aqua Marcia that also slaked Rome's thirst was ninety-one kilometres. As the flow of water depended entirely on gravity, the designers had to engineer a slope the entire length of the channel, not that you'd notice, as thanks to Roman ingenuity, their aqueducts had a gradient of approximately thirty-five centimetres per kilometre! That's roughly a mere one in three thousand.

Occasionally a much steeper gradient might be required because of the terrain, which would lead to faster flowing water that could cause erosion in a relatively short time. They solved this problem with the use of stepped inclines to reduce the force, or feeding the water into a huge, reinforced receiving tank, which would disperse the water pressure.

But that's not all the builders of these titans of ancient engineering had to contend with. In fact they had to go through hell and high water.

The magnificent Pont du Gard spanning the Gardon River in Southern France, part of a 50 km aqueduct supplying the Roman colony of Nemausus, which is present day Nimes. (Photo by Patrick Clenet.)

In some cases, to maintain the gradient it was necessary to circumvent mountains, or preferably tunnel through them.

Conduits were often buried and the water channels had to include regularly spaced sedimentation tanks to reduce the amount of impurities present in the water.

But perhaps the most enduring evidence of these great structures resulted when the Romans encountered a valley. The only way to get the water across was to build colossal double or even triple-arched bridges, many of which still span great valleys. The bridge supporting the aqueduct in Metz, France, for example, is over one kilometre long. The Pont du Gard, which supplied Nimes in France, is fifty metres and three arches in height, and is the best preserved such structure in the world - and is now a UNESCO World Heritage site. The Aqua Virgo (named after a young girl who directed thirsty soldiers to a spring which later supplied the water source) was built during the time of Emperor Augustus and astonishingly, is still in use today, supplying the water that tourists see gushing from Rome's Trevi Fountain and the fountains in the Piazza del Popolo.

The Roman Empire may have finally fallen in the fifth century, but its aqueducts continued to supply fresh water to people for more than a thousand years, helped in the development of agriculture and led to the building of towns and cities along their path, many of which still owe their existence to the genius of the original Roman engineers.

5
ARCHITECTURE

While most of the people in northern Europe were living in randomly sited, leaky huts made from timber, wattle and mud, the Romans were busy erecting colossal stone and concrete monuments to their gods, or for the purposes of government, and constructing towns of brick and mortar in straight lines, complete with sanitation, markets, storage facilities, theatres, paved roads and monumental necropoli for their dead. (See also Town Planning.) What we owe to the Romans in terms of architecture is incalculable. Just take a look around the centre of most towns or cities and you'll see the evidence. It's not that the Romans actually built the likes of Buckingham Palace or the British Museum in London, the Arc de Triomphe or the Louvre in Paris, the Brandenburg Gate in Berlin or the White House and U.S. Capitol in Washington, but their influence in clearly there for all to see. Greco-Roman architecture was the primary source of inspiration, for example, for Andrea Palladio, arguably the most influential architect in history. In particular, the famous Roman architect, Vitruvius, had a profound impact on Palladio's creativity, and you can hardly throw a rock in Italy without hitting one of his magnificent creations or something inspired by him and ancient Rome. The beautiful cities of Europe, North and South America and Australasia that we all wander about admiringly on our vacations, taking snaps of or selfies with them as a backdrop, are all a legacy of the long-dead, and often unknown, architects of the ancient world. It is true that the Romans borrowed a lot of their ideas from the Greeks, but it is also a fact that they developed and adapted their architecture into a separate style of their own, and it is this that became the primary source of inspiration for thousands of architects down the centuries.

It says something for Roman building techniques and styles, that besides their influence in the millennia to follow, many original Roman buildings are still intact, partially intact or in some cases, still in use. They took full advantage of new materials, particularly concrete (See also Concrete), and employed new technologies such as the arch and dome to construct exceedingly strong and enduring structures.

The Pantheon in Rome is a particularly good example. Originally a pagan temple, it was wisely adapted for use as a church in the seventh century by Pope Boniface IV, and has been the Church of St. Mary and the Martyrs ever since, thus saving it from the destruction that was often visited upon other Roman buildings in the succeeding centuries. Its famed dome was copied and reproduced countless times in the western world and was highly influential in the work of the architect Brunelleschi when he designed the towering dome of the Santa Maria del Fiore in Florence.

Almost two millennia after it was built the Pantheon's roof remains the largest unreinforced concrete dome in the world, a truly staggering achievement.

The stunning Pantheon building in Rome has stood for more than 1,800 years, complete with the world's largest unreinforced concrete dome. (Photo by Colin C. Murphy)

ANOTHER FINE EXAMPLE of their architectural skill is Castel Sant'Angelo, the towering edifice on the banks of the Tiber. Originally erected by Hadrian as his final resting place, its cylindrical shape was at the time the tallest structure in Rome and one of the highest in the world. Two millennia later it is still in use – as a National Museum.

And there are countless more such structures to be seen and admired all over Europe. So whenever you're passing your local courthouse, church or library, spare it more than a passing glance, as the chances are its style has drawn inspiration from the mind of one of Rome's long-forgotten architects, to whom we owe and enormous debt of gratitude.

6

BIRTHDAY CAKE

Next time you find yourself sitting around a table singing 'Happy birthday to you' and then watching as the birthday boy or girl blows out the candles and then begins to slice into that Black Forest Gateau or that Iced Coffee Cake, remember that you've the Romans to thank for this deliciously sinful tradition. Yes, when they weren't busy feeding Christians to lions or crucifying runaway slaves, they liked to celebrate birthdays with a cake dotted (possibly) with candles. The Romans can't take credit for the candle tradition though - that was the Greeks. They liked to honour Artemis, who was goddess of the hunt and the moon, by decorating a cake with candles to make it as bright as the moon. The Romans may or may not have borrowed the candle idea, but they certainly originated the birthday cake, although only to honour males. The girls had to wait until the twelfth century before their birthdays became a source of celebration.

A slice of Plăcintă cake, from Eastern Europe, which is similar to the original Roman birthday confection. (Photo by Nicubunu).

The Roman fare has the unfortunate name of *placenta cake*, from the Greek word *plakóenta* meaning 'flat', and the love poet Ovid even referred to the cake as part of the celebration of his brother's birthday in his book 'Tristia':

And now what?
You want the kind of coddling you usually get?
A white robe over my shoulders?
A pretty little smoking altar surrounded
by fresh flowers?
Grains of sacred incense crackling in the fire?
And me making little birthday cake offerings
with my head bowed
Moving my mouth in a prayer to you
to beg for something, something, good to happen

Placenta consists of layers of dough interspersed with cream cheese, nuts, honey and bay leaves and then baked, after which it is topped off with more honey. Sounds quite delicious! Although if you decide to bake it and serve it, perhaps you should introduce it as 'Roman Birthday Cake' and not 'placenta'.

Just a suggestion.

7

BOUND BOOKS

Before the advent of the codex (a book constructed of layered sheets of material bound together in some fashion), the principal form of document was the continuous scroll, which dates back to the earliest days of ancient Egypt. The only other forms of record keeping were stone tablets or flat pieces of wood inscribed with a burning tool, which weren't really practical options to carry around with you, or to amend on a regular basis.

The scroll had its problems, though, the main one being storage, and the limit to the length of each individual document, meaning that a book would often require multiple scrolls to fit its contents. Also, their looser, unenclosed nature made them more vulnerable to deterioration.

Along come the Romans, and in particular one Julius Caesar, who needed something much handier in which to write his '*Veni, vidi, vici*,' and his reflections on gutting and beheading about a million Gauls. Actually the Romans had bound books before Caesar came along, but they were made of thin sheets of wax-covered wood. Caesar wanted something easier to handle and store, and with more capacity, so he turned to the idea of binding papyrus.

It was the Egyptians who came up with papyrus, the first known form of paper, produced by taking the pith (tissue within the stems) of the papyrus plant that grew along the Nile, then crushing, flattening and drying it. Caesar commanded someone to take multiple sheets of papyrus and sew them together along the left hand edge, and hey presto, the world's first book in a form we would recognise.

When writers such as Martial (first century AD) encountered the new development they were keen to extol its virtues, believing it convenient and concise, and handy for taking on long journeys. The scroll had had its day, and within a century it had all but disappeared. Papyrus also began to fade into memory, replaced with parchment made from stretched and dried animal skin, which was much more durable.

The ninth century Codex Vaticanus Latinus was copied from a third century model, giving us an insight into the ancient Romans' book binding techniques.
(Photo: Anonymous)

When the Christians arrived in Rome a few centuries later, they were quick to recognize the codex as an efficient means of recording the bible and disseminating their creed, and the bound book's future was secure. And although glue and paper are the main materials used in books nowadays, the principal is still the same, and even digital books often still take on the form of the bound book, with the illusion of bound pages turning from the left-hand side.

Caesar's innovation certainly was a turn-up for the books.

8

BUREAUCRACY

To many people who've encountered some of the bureaucratic log jams or excessive form filling that seems to be endemic to the modern civil service (wherever you live,) the Romans are probably to be cursed rather than praised for the creation of the world's first bureaucracy. But the fact is that in any complex society, bureaucracy is a necessary evil, essential to the maintenance of order, although admittedly it can appear that it results in maintaining disorder.

Roman bureaucracy originated fairly early in the city's existence. As it began to expand from a small settlement on the Tiber out into the entire Italian peninsula, the powers that be realised that they would need an extensive network of record-keepers, census takers and tax collectors if they were to maintain control of their new state.

So around the mid-third century BC, the Republic created new high-level magistracies called *praetorships* and *quaestorships*, who were given the task of supervising provinces, (the term 'province' originally meant the scope of one's responsibility rather than a geographical area). These in turn each had a small army of minions to help them keep the books, ensure that taxes made their way to Rome, maintain a record of the citizenship, legal matters, and of state property and so on.

Bureaucracy carved in stone. The inscription reads: "By the decision of the Emperor Caesar Vespasianus Augustus, the tribune T. Suedius Clemens, having examined the documents and controlled the areas, restored the public areas occupied by private persons to the civic administration of Pompeii"
(Photo by René Voorburg)

BY THE TIME the first emperor, Augustus, came along (27 BC - 14 AD), the numbers working in Rome's central administration had reached five thousand or more, which is astonishing given that even medium-sized towns at the time might not have equalled that number in population terms. Having said that, the number of bureaucrats was so great because the empire had expanded to such a large extent that it required a quarter of a million soldiers to maintain and protect it, and two centuries later there were almost half a million men in the army, every one of who had to be provided with pay, rations, weapons and armour.

And besides keeping tabs on the army, Rome itself had grown to such an extent that its population was approximately one million, a staggering figure at the time. Luckily for Romans on the Italian peninsula, taxation had been abolished in 167 BC, so there was no need to chase down every baker and blacksmith for his ten sesterces in tax, yet all of these people still had to be documented in a census, building and land records had to be maintained, as did matters of law, all of which demanded a vast bureaucracy – and one which, to a large extent, seemed to have worked with reasonable efficiency. They did keep the place running for almost a thousand years, after all.

The practices of the Roman bureaucrats were of course mimicked when the empire fell, as once again the Christian church was happy to adopt the ways of their former pagan enemies, helping Christianity to spread far and wide, and to ensure that funds were levied and regularly paid in tribute back to Rome. Slowly bureaucratic systems evolved and developed over the centuries, but there are even today echoes of the original Roman system in our modern world, a prime example being the census.

So then next time you're on the phone for the fifth time yelling to a disinterested civil servant that you've been waiting six months for your application for a double-glazing grant to be processed, don't blame him, blame the Romans.

CALENDAR

Although the Gregorian calendar is the one we use today to tick off our birthdays, arrange to meet friends in the local bar or schedule a trip to a football game, we once more have Julius Caesar to thank for the first stab at producing a calendar of reasonable accuracy, and Julius and his underlings did a good job, as it only lost thirteen days over a period of 1,500 years. Incidentally, when they switched over from the Julian to the Gregorian in 1582, Protestants thought it was a Popish plot to undermine them and rejected it. Furthermore, when Protestants finally did adopt the new system around 1750, there were accounts of riots in England, with people taking to the streets to demand the thirteen days of their lives back!

But back to Julius Caesar. By the time he became dictator in 49 BC, the famed Roman realised that the seasons were completely out of kilter. People were forced to wear extra layers of clothing at a time of year when the sun was shining and the tulips were blossoming.

The original Roman calendar was based on moon cycles, but complicated further by the fact that the Romans considered even numbers unlucky, so every month was assigned either 31 or

29 days, with the one exception being February at 28. (Incidentally, they also believed that the left side was bad luck - the Latin for left is 'sinister' - and left-handers were considered bad news.) This all added up to just 355 days, so to compensate for that they added an extra month every two years called Mercedonius. But this didn't compensate with any level of accuracy, so Caesar decided enough was enough and hired an astronomer called Sosigenes to sort out the mess.

A Roman third century pictorial calendar from El Jem, North Africa, (the central twelve panels are the months) showing scenes from farming life, displayed now in Sousse Archaeological Museum, Tunisia. (Photo by Colin C. Murphy)

The Alexandrian based his calendar entirely on the Earth's revolutions around the sun. It takes our planet on average, 365 days, 5 hours, 48 minutes and 45 seconds to complete one full orbit. Now Sosigenes didn't measure it quite that accurately as he didn't have access to a digital clock, but he made what you'd have to say is a decent go of it, measuring a solar year at 365 days and 6 hours. So he was out by roughly 11 minutes, and it took one and half millennia before this had accumulated to an extent where someone noticed. So full marks to Sosigenes given the technology available to him at the time.

The resulting calendar introduced the world to the leap year, which would occur every four years, and fixed the number of days in each month to the same lengths they have now. Almost all of the months' names are also Roman in origin:

- January: Janus – the god of beginnings.
- February: Named after the purification ritual Februa, held on February 15th, which they believed drove evil spirits out of Rome.
- March: Mars – god of war.
- April: The origin is probably Roman, but it's uncertain. It may come from the verb 'aperire' meaning 'to open', as in spring buds opening, or it may derive from Aphrodite, the Greek goddess of love (Venus was the Roman equivalent).
- May: Named after the Greek goddess 'Maia', who the Romans re-named Bona Dea, the goddess of fertility.
- June: Juno – wife of Jupiter, the principal deity, and the goddess of marriage.
- July: Named in honour of Julius Caesar himself. Originally called Quintilis.
- August: Originally called Sextilis, it was renamed in 8 BC after Emperor Augustus.
- September: Its name derives from 'septem', which is Latin for 'seven', as it was originally the seventh month in the oldest known Roman calendar, the so-called 'Calendar of Romulus'.
- October: As with September, this derives from the

original Roman calendar, when it was the eighth month – from the Latin 'octo'.
- November: Another throwback to the Romulan calendar – from the Latin 'novem' meaning ninth.
- December: From the Latin 'decem' or tenth, as originally the tenth month of the old calendar.

So NEXT TIME you look at that fancy digital diary on your iPhone or the hanging calendar with pictures of cats on your kitchen wall, remember that if it hadn't been for the Romans, you wouldn't be able to organise your year with quite so much ease. Not in a month of Sundays.

10

CHRISTMAS

December 25th. A huge feast, the exchange of presents, the wine flowing, party games, a festival atmosphere. Sound familiar? No, it's not Christmas, it's Saturnalia, the Roman festival to honour Saturn, the god of the sun. Was this free-for-all party the precursor to the Christian celebrations that occurred in succeeding millennia? The answer is 'probably', and it almost certainly was a major influence.

Saturnalia was originally celebrated between December 17th and 19th, but people were enjoying themselves so much that it eventually expanded, and didn't end until December 23rd. It began as far back as 220 BC and was marked by a public banquet, the cancellation of public executions (which really is the ultimate seasonal gift) and a ban on declaring any new wars. By the time of Augustus, the Julian Calendar had seen the climax of Saturnalia shift to December 25th. And by now the traditions had also expanded to include being charitable to the poor, forgiving your enemies, being hospitable, party games, the exchange of gifts (usually in the form of pottery figures known as *sigillaria*) and the decoration of trees.

Classical artists loved to paint scenes of Roman festivals like Saturnalia as it gave then the excuse to depict lots of naked people behaving immorally. This one is called 'La jeunesse de Bacchus' by William-Adolphe Bouguereau. (Photo by leo.jeje)

Another aspect was that of role-reversal, when the masters of the house swapped clothes with the slaves and waited on tables for them, although you'd have to imagine that they didn't put up with too much of that. A Saturnalian monarch was also chosen by rolling dice in each household, and whose regal duties mainly involved directing festivities to make sure everyone was having a good time, especially himself. The Roman poet, Lucian of Samosata gives a sense of the activities in his poem 'Saturnalia':

'During my week the serious is barred: no business is allowed. Drinking and getting drunk, singing and games of dice, appointing of kings and feasting of slaves, dancing naked, clapping ... an occasional ducking of corked faces in icy water – such are the functions over which I preside.'

Which pretty much describes a lot of office Christmas parties.

Even when Christianity arrived in Rome, Saturnalia

continued to be observed. The Christians began to celebrate Christ's birthday around the middle of the fourth century but Saturnalia was still in full swing for as long as a century after that. When Rome finally fell in the fifth century, Saturnalia slowly slipped from human memory and was replaced by the annual celebration of Christmas on December 25th. But by then there can be little doubt that many of the traditions of one festival seeped across into the one that replaced it. For example, decorating trees has no religious Christian significance, but it was a Romans tradition and is something we still do two thousand years later.

Perhaps we should revive a few more of the ancient Roman traditions. Particularly the naked dancing.

11

CONCRETE

The Romans didn't invent concrete, that's a fact, but what they did invent was *Roman concrete*, which quite uniquely for the era, employed volcanic ash as a component, making it not only stronger, but also more durable, thereby preventing cracks forming as the seasons and temperatures changed. So impressive was Roman concrete, that modern chemists are still exploring its secrets as it was most probably stronger than the construction material we use nowadays.

The first known use of concrete was by Nabatean traders, who lived in a small area of what is now northern Saudi Arabia around 700 BC. They built houses with concrete floors and concrete water cisterns to help them survive in the desert. It was the use of concrete that allowed this race to exploit the desert and dominate the economic fortunes of the entire Arabian peninsula.

Some scientists are actually investigating if the Egyptians beat everyone to it however, and invented concrete two thousand years before the Romans began using it. Is it possible that the great pyramids were not constructed with giant carved blocks of stone, but that each block was in fact moulded in place using an early form of concrete? We'll get back to you on that one as the jury is still out, but for the moment it remains the belief that the pyramids were made from stone.

There is also evidence of small-scale use of early forms of concrete in Greece and Cyprus, but it was the Romans who actually realised the material's full potential when they began to use concrete to erect great edifices to their gods around 300 BC. Roman concrete furthermore was stronger than previous efforts and more resistant to wear and tear, which was particularly helpful if you lived in a region prone to earthquakes.

Perhaps the most famous Roman ruin is the Colosseum, which could hold 65,000 spectators and is largely intact. Its construction would not have been possible without the use of Roman concrete.
(Photo by Colin C. Murphy)

It was made by mixing quicklime, ground pumice and *pozzolana*, otherwise known as volcanic ash, and which takes its name from the town of Pozzuoli, where they mined the stuff. The Romans' use of this new wonder material is regarded as a turning point in the history of architecture. It allowed the construction of previously unimagined complex building forms that combined arches, domes and vaults – and on a grander scale than had ever been seen before. A couple of fine examples are the dome in Rome's Pantheon (see also Architecture) or the Colosseum, which they built in less than eight years and which could hold about 65,000 spectators, and is to a large extent, still standing, despite the intervention of centuries of earthquakes and stone thieves. Neither of these structures could have been erected using carved stone. The Baths of Caracalla are another truly impressive feat of architecture and demonstration of the use of Roman concrete. (See also Sanitation) The structure covers an area of 100,000 square metres and included a caldarium (hot room) and tepidarium (lukewarm room) along with a colossal colonnaded frigidarium (cold room) with a roof that was forty-five metres high, two gyms, a swimming pool, a maze of towering underground tunnels and a latrine house. Up to 1,600 people could use the baths at any one time. Such a structure would have been simply impossible but for the use of Roman concrete. The edifice even inspired the modern buildings of Pennsylvania Station in New York and Union Station in Chicago.

Just recently, scientists have discovered that Roman sea walls are far more durable than their modern counterparts because Roman concrete reacts with the seawater to form bonds that are as strong as the most resistant natural stone, whereas seawater has the opposite effect on modern Portland concrete, causing it to weaken and crumble after a number of decades.

The fact is that without their unique concrete, the Roman Republic or Empire might simply not have become the vast, powerful polity that it was. It allowed the Romans to expand their territories with the aid of roads and other infrastructure like housing, court and administration buildings and sanitation systems. And of course, probably of equal importance to those practical matters, who could not fail to be awed by the beauty and grandeur of Rome and the other cities it erected all over Europe? No wonder so many peoples were cowed by its sheer splendour.

It's easy to see why the Romans are said to have laid the foundations for so much of the architecture we see around us today.

12

FAST FOOD

Really? Was there a Burger King in ancient Rome? Cheeseburger, fries and a Pepsi please Marcus Flavius. Well, not quite. But long before Ronald McDonald or Burgerz 'R' Uz came along, the Romans were selling takeaway food that was designed to be served quickly and eaten there and then or on the same street.

Unlike the palatial Roman homes we're used to seeing recreated in movies and on TV, most citizens lived in cramped one or two room apartments with no cooking facilities. Their only option really was to eat out on the cheap. So next stop was the *thermopolium* (pl: *thermopolia*), a type of fast-food restaurant ubiquitous in Roman towns and cities. The name literally means 'place where hot food is sold'. Pompeii is a good example. The town had a population of about 12,000 people and there were 160 or more *thermopolia*. Imagine a small stadium holding 12,000 spectators having 160 fast-food outlets!

*The Thermopolium of Asellina in Pompeii, showing the counter in which the dolia were stored and the household shrine called a lararium, depicting Mercury and Dionysus, the gods of commerce and wine. Besides takeaway food, Asellina also satiated other appetites, as on the upper floor prostitutes entertained clients.
(Photo by Colin C. Murphy)*

You can still see plenty of well-preserved *thermopolia* in Pompeii and elsewhere in the ruins of ancient cities. They all took the same basic form (much in the way modern fast-food restaurants do) consisting of a room with a masonry counter opening on to the street, within which were sunken open jars called *dolia*, that were daily filled with foodstuffs like nuts, cheese, porridge, bread, fish, meat and honey, the food served in small jars or on plates, and usually eaten with the fingers or a spoon. Wine or other drinks like honeyed water were also available. A small minority of *thermopolia* had a room inside with a few tables or benches, but in general they operated as fast-food joints for the poor, where people could have a quick meal while leaning on the counter or take away handfuls of nuts or bread to eat on the go. Some of the establishments were decorated with small mosaics or frescoes featuring the likes of the god of commerce, Mercury or Bacchus, the god of wine.

Last but not least we should mention that other snack food beloved of Romans visiting their local *thermopolium* – stuffed dormice. They were caught in the wild in the autumn when they were at their fattest, skinned and stuffed with things like nuts, ground meat and spices, and then roasted and often served coated in honey.

But relax; it's unlikely the McDormouse will ever catch on.

13

GOVERNMENT

The Romans didn't invent democracy, that's true, but it was in the Roman Republic that the ideals of the system came to fruition and evolved to a level that, to this day, inspires many aspects of modern democratic government.

The term 'democracy' comes from the Greek words '*demos*' meaning 'common people' and '*kratos*' meaning 'strength.' In 508 BC, an ancient Greek lawgiver called Cleisthenes initiated the first democracy, and he is rightly lauded as the 'Father of Democracy.' But Rome's wasn't far behind. And its republic's beginnings are found not in any grand ideal to give power to the people, but in a rather tragic event.

It was 509 BC. The last king of Rome, Lucius Tarquinius Superbus, had a reputation as a tyrannical monarch, but it took the spark of one of his son's (Sextus Tarquinius) misdeeds to finally draw the curtain on the royal era. A noblewoman called Lucretia renowned for her beauty and virtue, was sleeping in her chamber one evening when Sextus broke in and raped her under threat of death. Worse was to come as soon after, shamed by what had happened, Lucretia stabbed herself through the heart.

When word got out, ordinary Romans were outraged – this was the spark that lit the fires of revolt and soon after Superbus was dethroned. Sextus fled into exile but was murdered there in revenge for his action.

Romans vowed that never again would they be ruled by a king, and thus began five centuries of a limited, although evolving form of democracy. Many of the former king's functions were transferred to two consuls, who served a term of one year, each having the power of veto over the other. This was one of the first of many checks and balances in Roman government to ensure one man could not simply exercise his own will unchecked – something that is common now among almost all democratic societies. Another elected official called a *tribune* also had the power of veto over the decisions of the senate. The Romans originated the power of veto, a concept that is widespread nowadays.

During the early decades of the Republic, about fifty wealthy patrician families were the dominant force in politics, with the common people, or *plebeians,* having little or no say or representation in matters of state. It was these families who occupied most of the seats in the Roman Senate. The *plebeians* were excluded from magistracies and religious positions and could not be elected as consul – yet they were still expected to take up arms and defend Rome in times of war. But as the decades moved by, this slowly began to change, and by 342 BC, laws passed by the senate had expanded their rights and stated that one of the two consuls must come from the ranks of the plebs. Among the more famous plebeians to be elected consul were Julius Caesar, Pompey Magnus and Mark Anthony. The notion that a person not of noble blood could ascend to the highest political office in the land is now enshrined in the democracies of the western world. Lech Wałęsa, for example, was a humble shipyard electrician in Poland who rose to become the country's president. Ramsay MacDonald came from an impoverished background, was the illegitimate son of a farm labourer, worked as a clerk, and became the first Labour Party politician to be elected as Prime Minister of the U.K.

The Roman government in action. A 19th century depiction of the Roman Senate by Cesare Maccari in which we see the great orator Cicero denouncing Cataline (far right), who was accused of a conspiracy to overthrow the state.
(1888. Palazzo Madama, Rome.)

Although Roman democracy was somewhat diluted when the Republic ended and the Empire was born in 27 BC, we were still left with a legacy that became the foundation model for many European and global democracies when the era of monarchies began to fade into memory. The United States, for example, has three branches of government that are strikingly similar to the Roman model. The Executive branch (or the Office of The President) resembles the elected Roman consuls. The Legislative branch (U.S. Congress) resembles the elected members of the

Roman Senate and the Judicial branch resembles the Roman *Praetors*, who were elected magistrates.

The Roman Republican government had created a system of the division of power that was unique in its time and which safeguarded against oppression by any single individual, and which has become an integral concept in the democracies of our modern world. And given the election of certain individuals to power in recent times, we should be eternally grateful for those checks and balances that we adopted from the ancient politicians of the Eternal City.

14

GUIDE DOGS

Although the formalised training of dogs to help blind people get around didn't begin until World War I, when the Germans began training the animals to assist blinded soldiers, there is evidence that the practice of employing dogs in this manner began with the Romans.

We certainly know that dogs were fairly commonplace in ancient Rome. A famous mosaic at the entrance to The House of the Tragic Poet in Pompeii depicts a snarling dog with the words 'Cave Canem' – Beware of the Dog. Another famous Pompeian dog was the unfortunate creature that was left chained outside a premises to guard it while his owner fled, only to be killed when Vesuvius erupted, his agonised form captured in a frozen moment of time forever.

The animals generally served as guard dogs, to kill vermin or as hunting dogs, but they were also kept as family pets. It's known that the Romans also used dogs to herd livestock, so they certainly knew the tricks to train an animal.

The badly damaged 'guide-dog' fresco from the House of Julia Felix in Pompeii, alongside a line-drawing rendition by Otto Keller from 1909. (Photo: Anonymous)

Given the Romans' other innovations, it shouldn't really be a surprise that someone figured out that a dog might be able to help a blind man get around. And we have direct evidence of this from a mural found in the House of Julia Felix in Pompeii. Besides the usual depictions of gods and mythology, the house proved a boon for archaeologists and historians in that it also featured multiple murals depicting the everyday life of ordinary citizens. They show people buying and selling goods in the marketplace, craftsmen plying their trade, magistrates pronouncing on matters of law and also - a woman giving alms to a blind man who is being led by a dog.

Like the guide dog, it seems the Romans led the way to a practice that is now commonplace all over the world.

15

INTERNATIONAL CURRENCY

History has thrown up a number of international currencies down the centuries, i.e. a currency that can be used to buy goods in more than one country. The Spanish Silver Dollar was one such, which was exchangeable for goods or services in the Spanish territories in the Americas, Spain, obviously, and in parts of Asia. The Pound Sterling also had an international presence, and at one point could be used in Australia, India, Ireland, New Zealand and South Africa. The United States Dollar, while only enjoying a limited overseas usage, still has had a huge international influence as international exchange rates were once pegged to the U.S. dollar, and many national currencies still are. It is estimated that about half of all financial transactions in the world are done in U.S. dollars, so it really is not just a national but also an international currency. But in terms of the man or woman in the street buying their shopping with cash, the only currency that can be used on a wide international scale is the Euro, which is used in some nineteen different countries.

Yet even the Euro's widespread usage pales into insignificance beside Roman currency, which introduced the idea to the world of taking a sesterce minted in the north of England and using it to by a mug of wine in Mesopotamia, or modern day Iraq. Were it still in circulation today, you would be able to use a sesterce or denarius in any one of about forty countries, from the westernmost parts of the Iberian Peninsula to eastern Turkey to the deserts of Northern Africa and all the way north to Britain.

A reproduction of a sacrifice at the Temple of Moneta, near which Roman currency was minted, and which gives us the word 'money'. (From 'Everyday Life in Ancient Rome by F. R. Corwell, 1961. Illustration by J. Buhlmann and A. von Wagner.)

THE ROMANS BEGAN to use minted coinage in the fourth century BC, replacing a system of barter, and the actual origin of the words 'mint,' 'money' and 'monetary' come from a temple dedicated to Juno Moneta, the goddess of funds, that was beside the workshop in Rome that manufactured silver coinage. As Rome expanded into a vast global empire, it took its currency with it and tribespeople in northern Europe used to exchanging things like eggs for a hatchet, suddenly found themselves handling metal coins like the *as*, the *sesterce*, the *denarius*, and if they were very fortunate, the *aureus*.

Thanks to the longevity and great expanse of the Roman state, their currency continued to live on even after the empire collapsed, in some cases right up to the Middle Ages, and was the model used for the subsequent currencies of many European and Arabic states. The names of some Roman coins even survive today, such as the Arabic dinar (*denarius*), and older British readers might recall pounds, shillings and pence, or L.s.d. for short, which is an abbreviation of the Roman denominations *librae, solidi* and *denarii*.

So ubiquitous were Roman coins across Europe, the Middle East and North Africa that there are literally millions of them still down there beneath our feet and you can buy a handful of them on eBay for less than the price of a few drinks in a bar. On the other hand, some of the rarer Roman coins are worth a pretty penny, the current world record held by a gold *aureus* depicting Emperor Maxentius, which sold for one and a half million dollars! As a piece of ancient graffiti in Pompeii reads – '*Pecunia non olet*' or 'Money doesn't stink.'

That sort of money certainly doesn't.

16

LANGUAGE & PHRASES

When you think of the Latin language you probably associate it with the names of plants or animals as they appear in scientific tomes e.g. *Canis lupus familiaris* (dog) or *quercus robur* (common oak tree). Another place you might encounter it is in religion, particularly the Catholic Church e.g. *Corpus Christi* (Body of Christ) or *Gloria in excelsis* (glory in the highest). Latin also occasionally pops up in Hollywood movie titles such as 'Ad Astra' (To the Stars), 'Ex Machina' (From the Machine) or 'John Wick 3 - Parabellum' which is borrowed from the fourth century Roman adage 'Si vis pacem, para bellum,' that translates as, 'If you want peace, prepare for war.'

And then there are the mottoes. Countless organisations, schools, clans and governments employ Latin to give themselves a bit of gravitas. From golf clubs such as Royal Troon in Scotland - *Tam Arte Quam Marte*, (As much by skill as by strength) to superpowers like the U.S. – *E pluribus unum* (Out of many, one), to individual clans like Murphy – *Fortiset hospitalus* (Brave and hospitable) So true, that last one!

But other than those, many people tend to regard Latin as a dead language, as nobody uses it for everyday discourse anymore. Well, that's partly true. And partly untrue. It's not so much a dead language as one that has lived on in countless successive generations, that same way you inherited your big nose from your granddad or your tiny feet from your great grandmother.

It's the same reason when you're on your vacation somewhere in Europe you can usually make a stab at translating a sign or a menu, because so many of the words have the same roots in Latin. A brief demonstration of the durability of the language can be had from an examination of the words 'durable' and 'artist':

Latin *Durabilis Artista*
English *Durable Artist*
French *Durable Artiste*
Italian *Duravole Artista*
Spanish *Durable Artista*

You'll find hundreds, if not thousands of similar words in a multiplicity of European languages, including English, of course.

So if you've ever reached a quota (*L: quota*), had an abdominal (*L: abdomen*) ulcer (*L: ulcus*) felt animosity (*L: animus*), sniffed a rose (*L: rosa*), caught a mouse (*L: mus*), embraced (*L: brachium)* your mother (*L: mater*) or father (*L: pater*) or had a magnificent (*L: magnus*) canine (*L: canis*) friend (*L: amica*), then you've been speaking Latin in a roundabout way.

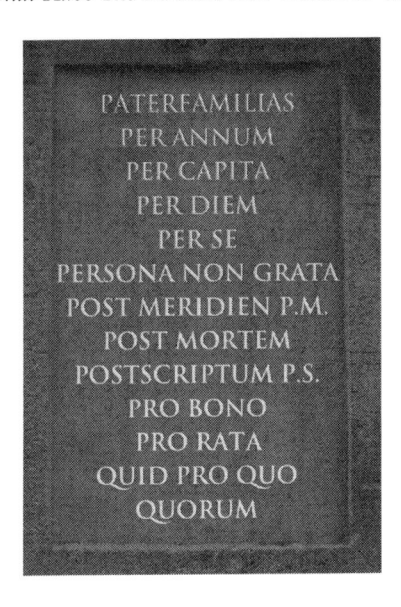

> PATERFAMILIAS
> PER ANNUM
> PER CAPITA
> PER DIEM
> PER SE
> PERSONA NON GRATA
> POST MERIDIEN P.M.
> POST MORTEM
> POSTSCRIPTUM P.S.
> PRO BONO
> PRO RATA
> QUID PRO QUO
> QUORUM

Dead language? Hardly. We use a great number of Latin phrases almost daily without a second thought. (Photo by Colin C. Murphy)

And besides the thousands of words in English with Latin genes, there are also a whole bunch of Latin phrases we use almost on a daily basis without a second thought.

> Have you established your *bona fides?*
> (With good faith.)
> Have you an *alibi*? (Elsewhere.)
> Gotten a *bonus*? (Good!)
> *E.g.* (*exempli gratia*: for the sake of example.)
> It's not this sentence *per se* that's important, but the Latin meaning. (In itself.)
> But let's finish with a little *quid pro quo*. (Something for something.)

So as not to upset the *status quo*, and make it one language *versus* another, here's a *verbatim* quotation: *vice versa* cannot be written *versa vice, i.e.* (id est) Latin does not deserve an *R.I.P.* (*requiescat in pace*).

Take it from a *homo sapiens*.

17
LAW

Ancient Rome left countless marks on today's world, but nowhere is this more evident than in our modern legal system, where its influence has been immense.

The earliest known drafted realisation of Roman law was seen in The Twelve Tables, which resulted from a long social struggle between *patricians* and *plebeians*. After the overthrow of the last king, Tarquinius Superbus, the *patricians* alone ruled the new Republic. Laws governing citizens were unwritten and interpreted only by a handful of *pontifices*, or patrician priests. As they tended to interpret the law to favour their own class, the common people soon began to demand a fairer system, which eventually led to the creation of laws that were literally carved in stone and known as The Twelve Tables. These were publicly displayed in the forum and set out the rights and duties of every citizen in terms of courts, trials, land rights, debt, and so on. The laws evolved over time to reflect the contemporary situation e.g. if Rome was at war, and were also affected significantly by the advent of the Empire, but the fundamentals remained the same.

Romans studying The Twelve Tables in the forum, setting out the basic rights and duties of all Romans.

When the Roman Empire collapsed, it continued in a sense as the Byzantine Empire, and in 529 AD, its Emperor Justinian I, decided to collect, clarify and update all of the ancient Roman laws, eradicating inconsistencies and contradictions and speeding up the legal processes. This major reform was known as the *Corpus Juris Civilis* or Body of Civil Law, and it became the basis for almost all European law for a millennium, and still exerts a profound influence on matters legal in virtually every country on the planet.

From weighty legal issues to the smallest of our modern rights, Roman law exerts a presence. You're probably aware, for example, that if you buy something like a microwave oven, take it home and it explodes, that you have legal recourse to claim your money back and force the seller to pay for any damage to your property or indeed, your person. That simple law of contract, exercised every day, can be traced all the way back to The Twelve Tables.

But that's a mere trifle. Here are a few more examples of legal concepts that find their foundation in Roman Law:

- The concept of a plaintiff, a defendant, legal representation and impartial judges are all aspects of the ancient legal system.
- Jury trials did not exist but in the Roman system a number of senators and knights or other prominent citizens were annually chosen by a praetor to act as his assessors, and some of these were appointed to sit in judgment with him. They would then accept a majority verdict of guilty or not guilty, making them in effect, juries, *per se*.
- As with today's statutes, under Roman law every citizen was afforded the following rights:
- The right of personal property.
- The right to vote (Roman law excluded women.)
- The legality of wills.
- The right of appeal.
- The right of the accused to a defence and to be innocent until proven guilty.
- The right to get married and divorce.
- The right to conduct a business.

All of which are principles that we pretty much take for granted in the modern era. And there are countless other laws and practices fundamental to 21st century law that are far beyond the scope of this book. If you want discover more, go and study to be a lawyer – Roman Law is still a mandatory subject for students in civil law jurisdictions.

There is one aspect of Roman Law that has definitely survived the ages. It is best summed up by the Roman writer Valerius Maximus, whose works come from the reign of Tiberius (14 - 37 AD). He remarked that laws are not unlike a spider's web in that they catch the weak (i.e. the poor) but let the strong (i.e. the rich) escape.

18

MAIL SERVICE

Although there is some evidence of a limited mail service in ancient Persia and India, the first definite and well-document manifestation of a service comparable to our understanding now, was the *Cursus Publicus*, (Public Way), which was created under Emperor Augustus (62 BC – 14 AD).

The service was limited to imperial officials and their associates, and officially was meant for state business, but naturally lots of people used it to send letters of a more personal nature. And the slaves of private individuals also availed of the mail system infrastructure to deliver letters and parcels to family, friends and business acquaintances abroad.

As the decades passed the *Cursus Publicus* came to be used by a broader number of people, and we know that lowly Roman soldiers could send letters home asking for their family to send various items - military garrison commanders, for example, would permit the ordinary ranks to send and receive letters alongside the official mail as a means of maintaining morale. A particularly amusing, and touching, example of this is found among the hundreds of postcard-sized letters, made of thin slivers of wood, that were recovered from the site of the northern British Roman fort at Vindolanda. There are many instances of letters complaining about the cold and the food and the dangerous Picts, and then there's this one, from a soldier to his mother in far-away Gaul:

'Paria udonum ab sattua solearum duo et subligariorum duo.'

Loosely translated that means 'Please send me socks, two pairs of sandals and two pairs of underpants!'

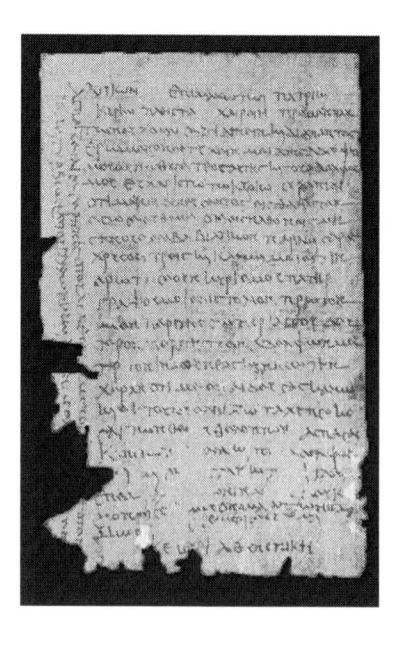

An actual letter from a soldier, Apion, sent all the way from Misenum (present day Miseno) to his father, Epimachos in Alexandria, Egypt, using the Roman mail service.
(Source: A History of the Early World by James H. Breasted, 1944.)

THE ROMAN MAIL service was feasible for one principal reason – the road network. (See also Roads). The Roman road network was vast, boasting about eighty thousand kilometres of paved roads. Its tentacles stretched to every corner of the empire. With the creation of the mail service, innumerable stations had to be built across the continent. These offered fresh horses, grooms, blacksmiths, food, accommodation and replacement mail couriers. Many of these were established locally, the owners then reimbursed by the state.

The Byzantine scholar Procopius gives us an (almost) contemporary account of how the service operated:

'The earlier Emperors, in order to obtain information as quickly as possible regarding the movements of the enemy in any quarter, sedition, unforeseen accidents in individual cities, and the actions of the governors or other persons in all parts of the Empire, and also in order that the annual tributes might be sent without danger or delay, had established a rapid service of public couriers throughout their dominion. As a day's journey for an active man they fixed eight 'stages,' or sometimes fewer. In every stage there were forty horses and many grooms. The couriers completed the work by using relays of fine horses, often covered in one day as great a distance as they would otherwise have covered in ten.'

It is estimated that using the system at its maximum efficiency, with horses galloping at full tilt between stages, urgent messages could travel in excess of 200 kilometres a day. And the system wasn't limited to letters. Larger, heavier parcels were sent using oxen to haul a cart.

Here's another touching example of a letter, written on papyrus that was despatched from what is modern day Budapest. It was sent by a Roman soldier called Aurelios Polion to his mother, brother and sister in Rome, and would have travelled the roads of the empire in a the saddlebag of a courier about 1800 years ago. Many of the sentiments could have been written today:

> 'I pray that you are in good health night and day. I do not cease writing to you, but you do not have me in mind. But I do my part writing to you always and do not cease having you in my heart. But you never wrote to me concerning your health, how you are doing. I am worried about you because although you received letters from me often, you never wrote back to me so that I may know how you are keeping.'

When the empire collapsed, the *cursus publicus* continued in use throughout much of the Byzantine period and became the blueprint for the development of future mail delivery systems in Europe and beyond.

But back to the poor cold soldier in Vindolanda. Caesar famously wrote '*Veni, vidi*' *vici*,' or 'I came, I saw, and I conquered,' which has in effect become his epitaph. A more fitting epitaph for that particular soldier might be 'I came, I saw, and I asked my mother to send underpants.'

19

MILITARY STRATEGY

Rome's military success has become a thing of legend. Their tactics, training, discipline, logistical organisation and so on, saw them enjoy far more victories than defeats. And the defeats, when they came, were often at the hands of enemies who were copying the very tactics that the Romans themselves had used in the past.

And while the Roman Empire did eventually fall after a thousand years, the strategies they employed would have an impact and influence on many an army in the centuries since.

To a large extent, Roman military tactics were forgotten for a very long time, and many a battle was fought during the Middle Ages between what were hordes of largely untrained and undisciplined men, who would clash in a field somewhere and hack each other to death head-on, the side with the most left standing at the end claiming victory. But then the Renaissance arrived around the fifteenth century and artists, architects and philosophers began to rediscover the treasures of the classical world. But besides buildings and sculptures, another legacy of the Romans began to re-emerge – their military genius.

Innumerable generals and political leaders around Europe

began to look at the Roman military model as the basis for their armies, making sure their men were thoroughly trained, introducing a meritocracy so that the better fighters and leaders, and not just the wealthiest, rose through the ranks, and by understanding that logistical support was just as vital as weaponry if you wanted victory.

Maurice, Prince of Orange, gives us a good example. He was the leader of the Dutch Republic in the early seventeenth century and one of the finest military strategists of the age. Maurice initiated a whole new school of military practice by reapplying ancient Roman tactics and innovating in the fields of logistics, training and by employing a professional army. And to great effect, as he led his armies to innumerable victories against Spain during the Eighty Years War.

Moving forward a few centuries, the legendary Napoleon was openly admiring of the ancient Romans, and besides his famed battle tactics, he created many symbolic connections between his army and those of Rome. His forces marched beneath eagle banners just as the Roman legions had, and he was responsible for edifices like the Arc de Triomphe, which imitated Emperor Constantine's arch in Rome, and the Vendome column, modelled on Trajan's column. He even commissioned a portrait depicting him bare-chested with his arm and legs draped in a toga and had coins minted showing him crowned with a Roman-style laurel wreath. Napoleon also mimicked the Roman military in terms of logistical support and training, and kept soldiers from allied satellite states in separate formations as support to the French citizen army – just as the Roman had, and used Roman tactics such as the military square to great effect.

Quintus Fabius Maximus Verrucosus, the originator of the Fabian Strategy, which has been mimicked countless times in history. (Sculpture: J. B. Hagenauer, Fabius Cunctator (1777) from the Schonbrunn Palace, Vienna. Photo by schurl50.)

But perhaps the greatest example of Roman strategy in history is the one that bears the name of the man who initiated it. Quintus Fabius Maximus Verrucosus gave the world the Fabian strategy. When Hannibal invaded Italy in 218 BC, his armies proceeded to inflict one heavy defeat after another on successive Roman armies, thanks to the Carthaginian general's tactical genius. Quintus Fabius Maximus was given the task of defeating the Carthaginian and rather than attack his enemy head-on, he adopted the strategy of a war of attrition, initiating constant minor skirmishes and then pulling back, disrupting supply lines, removing or even destroying supplies of food to starve the foraging army and wearing down morale. The strategy assumes one has time on one's side, which the Roman general did, as Hannibal was in a foreign, hostile land in constant need of fresh supplies.

Quintus Fabius Maximus's strategy was extremely successful, but unfortunately the Roman Senate and people were used to imposing quick, crushing defeats on their enemies, and began to lose faith in the tactics of patience. The Senate decided to replace him with Gaius Terentius Varro, who unfortunately led his armies into the greatest Roman defeat in history at the Battle of Cannae in 216 BC. Afterwards, the Senate realised the benefit of the Fabian strategy and adopted it once again to telling effect, and finally succeeded in driving Hannibal from Italy after a prolonged war.

The Fabian strategy was copied many times in the millennia that followed. The French general Bertrand du Guesclin employed it during the Hundred Years War against the English. The British were also on the receiving end of the tactic during the American Revolutionary War, when George Washington used it to great effect, earning him the nickname 'The American Fabius'. Napoleon, ironically a great fan of Roman strategy, had the tables turned on him when the Russians employed a Fabian strategy in the defence of their homeland. And even in the twentieth century, the Vietnamese Independentists successfully used a Fabian strategy against the vastly better equipped French during the First Indochina War.

Although the Empire may have foundered fifteen hundred years ago, in many ways the Romans continue to win battles right up to the present day.

20

POLITICAL CAMPAIGNING

You're familiar with the story. An election is called. Politicians of different shades appear from the woodwork and start promising you all sorts of goodies if you'll vote for them. Election messages start to appear everywhere proclaiming a particular guy's attributes, his generosity, his trustworthiness, his virtues as a family man, a man of the people. And then after a while the mud-slinging starts. You begin to hear and see nasty things about certain candidates. He's a liar, a traitor, he doesn't care about the people, just himself. Or he has some seedy secrets from his past that disqualify him as a candidate.

Of course, we're not talking about a modern-day election here, we're talking about the elections that took place in Pompeii two thousand years ago! One of the great legacies of Pompeii's rediscovery were the thousands of messages left on the town's walls by its inhabitants, politicians and their supporters included. And undoubtedly this was reflective of countless other towns in the Roman world, including Rome itself, in which some examples also survive. When an election was in the offing, the gloves were off no matter where you were in the Republic or Empire.

Here are a few examples of political campaigning, ancient-style, from Pompeii, which has hundreds of such slogans. In many ways, they're no different from what we see now.

The pair below are going to look after the town's infrastructure and are also very honourable gents, or so they claim:

I beg you to elect Quintus Marius Rufus and Marcus Epidius Sabinus aediles in charge of streets, sacred and public buildings; they are worthy.
Onesimus was the whitewasher.

The same man, Marcus Epidius, pops up in the next one also, by now campaigning for a position higher than *aedile*, that of *duumvir*, or head of the town council. Judging by his election slogan, he's a paragon of virtue:

I ask you to elect Epidius Sabinus duumvir with judicial power. He is worthy, a defender of the colony, and in the opinion of the respected judge Suedius Clemens and the council, because of his services and uprightness, worthy of the municipality. Sabinus, the theatre official, supports him with applause.

This chap invokes the blessing of the gods in his bid, a familiar tactic nowadays, especially in the U.S.

I ask you to elect Numerius Barcha as duumvir, a good man, and may Pompeian Venus be favourable to your offerings.

The fellow below is an absolute saint, if you can believe his electoral machine:

Gaius Cuspius for aedile. If honour is bestowed on a man who lives modestly, to this young man ought the glory he deserves be given.

And this candidate promises to put food in the mouths of the hungry:

*I beg you to elect Gaius Julius Polybius aedile.
He brings good bread!*

*A 2000 year-old political campaign from Pompeii -
The Thermopolium of Asellina bears a great many slogans,
including:*
Elect Gnaeus Sabinus aedile, worthy of office.
Elect C Julius Polybius duumvir, Zymrina begs.
Elect C Lollius duumvir for roads and temples. I beg of you.
(Photo by Colin C. Murphy)

But then it turns nasty. Just like today, a politician's supporters were not only keen to promote him as a positively wonderful chap, but also to rubbish the reputation of his opponents. To that end they sent out sign-writers to undermine their enemies. The following are a few of the many examples of negative campaigning evident in Pompeii.

> *All the deadbeat layabouts ask for Vatia as aedile!*

> *The late night drinkers ask you to elect Marcus Cerrinius Vatia aedile.*

> *Elect Caius Lollius Fuscus duumvir for looking after the roads and the sacred and public buildings. Aselina's whores ask you this.*

> *The petty thieves support Vatia for the aedileship!*

> *The fugitive slaves ask for Marcus Cerrinius Vatia as aedile!*

And one last rude one, although the candidate, one Isidore, probably wouldn't adopt this colourful line as his favoured election slogan...

> *Vote Isidore for aedile; he's the best at licking c...!*

Ok, today's campaigns wouldn't be as un-PC as that, but in all other respects, very little has changed in two thousand years when it comes to politicians trying to get our votes.

21

ROADS

At face value, it's hard to imagine how roads built by the Romans could exert any influence that's still visible today. After all, most of the roads the Romans built have vanished and we use completely different materials and methods to build our modern road infrastructure (which doesn't have a fraction of the longevity of Roman roads). But let's take a closer look.

Before the Roman state began to expand outward into Europe in the fifth century BC, there was no such thing as a paved road. What byways there were consisted almost exclusively of hard-packed earth, and these were few and far between. Even in the early days of expansion, the Romans didn't pave roads outside the city, although they did improve them with better drainage, signage, the addition of bridges and so on. But that all began to change in 312 BC, when a censor named Appius Claudius Caecus began construction of what was then considered a thing of wonder – a paved road 563km long – and which to this day bears his name: the Appian Way or Via Appia.

Although construction methods and materials might vary depending on the terrain, there were certain basics to which all

Roman roads adhered after the Appian Way. A shallow trench was dug along the route of the road and this was then filled in with multiple layers. First came a layer of sand, then one of crushed rock, then one of mortar, then one of gravel mixed with cement and finally a layer of paving stones. The centre of the road sloped down towards the sides to allow water to run off into drainage ditches. The roads were all a minimum of three metres wide but broader where a curve was necessary, and could be up to five metres wide depending on whether it was a military or trade route. They were also designed to be as straight as possible to minimize construction material in the short term, and travel times in the long term. It's a startling fact that 62km of the Via Appia is still in use, mostly by pedestrians, and that it is the longest stretch of straight road in Europe.

*A section of the original Via Appia outside Rome.
62km of the road is still in use today.
(Photo by Colin C. Murphy)*

Roman engineers preferred to go through or over obstacles rather than to circumvent them, so ravines were bridged and hills tunnelled. These massive excavations could be up to a kilometre long – in fact the longest Roman road tunnel is the Cocceius tunnel near Naples, built in 38-36 BCE, and because of its extraordinary (for its time) length, also had ventilation shafts built into the design. This tunnel is still viable and at the time of writing is due to reopen to the public after some restoration works in recent years.

You may have heard of the expression 'All roads lead to Rome', which makes perfect sense when you see the extent to which the network of roads grew. Towards the end of the Empire, there were 80,000 km of paved roads in Europe and a further 300,000 km unpaved. 372 great roads connected all the provinces and principal cities of the empire and 29 main roads extended out from Rome like a colossal spider's web. And at the networks' peak, you could travel from the north of England to the north of Sudan without ever straying from a Roman road.

But back to the question of the legacy of those roads in today's world. Well, archaeologists have long recognised that a great number of the principal routes and highways we use today were built over the original paths of Roman roads. Many popular routes in France, Britain, Spain and Germany directly follow the original Roman plan, and there is still visible evidence of the roads to be seen occasionally. But scientists now believe that the influence of Roman roads was even greater than previously assumed. When they overlaid an image of the network over a satellite image of Europe by night, there was a remarkable affiliation between the routes of the roads and the lights from Europe's principal cities and towns. In other words wherever there was a road, or certainly a road junction, a town or village tended to spring up, and most of those settlements have grown into our modern day conurbations.

And one last thing about those ancient thoroughfares. Roman roads did not get potholes or crack with a hard frost, had perfect drainage and were rarely washed away in floods, and they're still usable after two millennia. The estimated lifespan of a modern asphalt road is twenty years. Perhaps our engineers should take a leaf out of the ancients' book, not to mention some of their designs.

22

SANITATION

The use of sewerage systems and a controlled water supply predates the foundation of Rome by about two thousand years, as there is evidence of such works to be found in the Indus Valley in Asia. But it was the Romans who elevated sanitation to a social and cultural imperative and took it to a level that would influence city designers far into the future.

The Romans loved water more than most peoples of the world. They had seven either major or minor gods devoted to water. They loved fresh water spouting from their springs, they liked the sight of fountains gushing forth all over their cities and towns, they appreciated the use of water to flush away their excrement, and most of all they loved to bathe. Every self-respecting Roman town had at least one public baths. Pompeii alone had five bathing institutions.

But while those ancients appreciated the social and cleansing aspects of bathing and sanitations, they unfortunately hadn't a clue when it came to bacteria. As a result, despite the presence of advance sanitation systems, Rome and other cities of the age were often plagued with disease. Mind you, compared to some later cities of the Middle Ages, Roman towns were like pristine, bleached, germ-free paradises.

For a complex sanitation system to function, the very first thing you need, obviously, is a supply of water. Lots and lots of it. As early as 312 BC, Rome realised that its water supply was inadequate, despite it straddling the Tiber and the presence of multiple springs within the city walls. These sources were badly polluted, so up stepped the man who was also responsible for Rome's famed Via Appia, the censor Appius Claudius Caecus. He commissioned the building of the city's first aqueduct, the Aqua Appia. As Rome continued to expand, more and more were needed, so that by the time of Caesar's assassination in 44 BC, there were four aqueducts supplying the city, each of them colossal infrastructural achievements. Leap forward to the third century AD and there were eleven, with a combined length of over 800 km. So where was all that water going?

Roman latrines are almost a thing of legend now, and a source of mirth for modern observers. Unlike the present-day attitude of strict modesty and privacy concerning one's bodily waste, the Romans saw a visit to the latrine as a means of socialising and catching up on the latest gossip. And there seems to have been little or no separation of the sexes in the much-frequented public latrines that you can still visit in the ruins of many Roman towns. The famously immodest Romans saw a visit to the latrine as a bodily function no different to blowing one's nose. Waste from the latrines was then flushed away by piped water that swept it into the sewers.

Rome's sewerage system was another marvel of engineering. Its most famous sewer was the Cloaca Maxima, which was originally begun by the Etruscans, Rome's predecessors in the region. But at that stage it was merely an open drain. It is named after Cloacina, the goddess of the sewers (yes, Rome even had a goddess who presided over the sewers!) As the city developed, later Roman engineers covered the sewer with an arched roof, and incredibly, it is still functioning in its original capacity, serving the present day area of the Roman Forum and the surrounding hills. It is the longest functioning sewer in the world. By 100 AD a complex web of sewers had evolved beneath the citizens' feet and many of the wealthier homes were connected directly to the system.

The problem was that not everyone was, and the poorer citizens who weren't near a public latrine, or couldn't be bothered, tended to throw their waste out into the street, creating enormous health hazards. Eventually a law had to be passed banning this practice during daytime because of the number of unsuspecting citizens who were literally dumped on! Ultimately your wealth, or lack of it, was a key factor in your health, thanks to the rich enjoying better and more immediate access to public sanitation. For the unfortunates who inhabited Rome's slums, the hazards, odours and unsightliness of frequently dumped faeces must have been near intolerable.

But then there was always the opportunity to have a bath. Great, you'd think, at least you could wash that filth away on a daily basis. Well, sort of.

Roman bathing facilities were pretty much ubiquitous – every town had at least one. Bathing was not simply a matter of stripping, climbing into a pool of water and scrubbing yourself down. Thanks to Roman engineering genius, the typical bathhouse featured three separate rooms. You started off in the *tepidarium*, which as it suggests, wasn't overly hot. In many cases there was no water in this room, which was heated by an underfloor system call a *hypocaust* (See also Variety – Central Heating.) Next you moved through in the *caldarium*, which was a very hot room with a bathing area. Having lolled about naked chatting to your fellow citizens about the chariot races, the price of bread or the recent beheadings in the forum, you then passed into the room called the *frigidarium*. And yes, it was as cold as it sounds. Here you briefly plunged your entire body into an icy cold pool. Very refreshing. Some bathhouses also had a dedicated steam room, just like nowadays, called a *sudatorium*, which was a vaulted sweating room, and which was also followed by a dip in the *frigidarium* pool. The Arabic and Turkish love of steam rooms has its roots here, as they adopted the Roman concept as their own when they eventually overran the Eastern Roman Empire.

*A cross-section of the stunning
Baths of Diocletian, as illustrated by French artist
Edmond Jean-Baptiste Paulin. (1880)*

The largest single bathing facility was The Baths of Diocletian completed in 306 AD, and along with the usual rooms described above, the complex housed a large semi-circular theatre, gymnasiums, a library, elaborate gardens, and a 3,500 square metre swimming pool. It was highly decorated in marble and its walls adorned with beautiful frescoes and mosaics. The baths could host 3,000 bathers at any one time, with which even the grandest modern bathing facilities would struggle to compete. Incidentally, during the Republican period, bathing was generally segregated between the sexes, with women having separate (and smaller) facilities and times of attendance to men. However during the Empire, attitudes became quite relaxed and mixed bathing became the norm.

So you'd imagine that you'd emerge from all that as clean as a whistle. Not so. The warm, moist atmosphere in a Roman bath was an ideal breeding ground for germs and parasites. When people come into contact with the water through swimming, bathing or drinking, infection spreads like wildfire. Anyone going to the baths with an open cut could easily emerge cleansed without, but gangrenous within. And because the water wasn't changed too regularly, by the end of its use it was essentially a pool of liquid sweat, grime, excrement, urine and semen. (Better not to ask.) The Romans were actually aware of this on one level, as when the bell would sound for the opening of the baths, there was a rush to get there as early as possible so you could plunge into the newly changed and relatively clean water.

A great deal of the understanding of the benefits of cleanliness was lost in the Middle Ages, and the Roman baths allowed to fall into ruin - in effect they threw the baby out with the bath water. And the people who inhabited towns of that era would have been foul smelling, filthy and unsanitary. But once again, as new cities started to rise and expand post-Renaissance, scholars began to study the sanitation systems of antiquity, and based many of their sewerage and water-supply systems on those of the ancient engineers. Some of the sewers beneath our feet were actually constructed in Victorian times, and these were inspired directly by Roman designs. And when it comes to bathing, many of the spas and large bathing *thermae* that became popular in parts of Europe in the eighteenth and nineteenth centuries (Budapest alone has seven) directly follow the Roman model, and featured tepid, hot and cold pools. Luckily these facilities are treated with chlorine and the water changed on an on-going basis. Many have even taken the Roman influence further by housing the baths in classical revival architecture, so you can really get a sense of what an ancient Roman felt like when he or she took a trip to the baths, although unlike the Romans, in all likelihood you would probably keep your togs on.

But last word on Roman bathing we'll leave to the great statesman, orator and philosopher, Cicero, who wrote:

> *'The gong that announced the opening of the public baths each day was a sweeter sound than the voices of the philosophers in their school.'*

23

TIMEKEEPING

We have the ancient Egyptians to thank for the hour, which concept they originated about 2000 BC. And although the Romans didn't invent the hour, they did introduce the world to the 12-hour cycle, which occurred twice every day. They also were the first to introduce the concept of each new day beginning at midnight at the end of the previous day, which gave us the terms 'a.m.' and 'p.m.', evident in the fact that they are the Latin phrases *'ante-meridiem'* and *'post-meridiem'* meaning 'before noon' and 'after noon' respectively.

Roman timekeeping was initially judged by the sundial, something they imported from Sicily in 263 BC. But sundials had to be adjusted in different latitudes and had the other obvious disadvantage that they didn't work in overcast conditions or at night. They soon adopted the ancient Egyptian system of using water clocks, which could be calibrated using a sundial. The clock was known as the *clepsydra*, from the Greek 'water thief' and in its simplest form was a container with a small hole in the base, usually marked with the hours of the day as the water diminished. But the Romans also developed much more complex versions of this and the great architect Vitruvius (See also: Architecture) described a 'water alarm clock'!

The increasing complexity of these devices is evident from Vitruvius's own description of one of the simpler forms:

... the hours are marked on a pilaster - a figurine indicates them in turn with a wand throughout the day. The shortening and lengthening of the days must be corrected daily and monthly with the addition or removal of wedges. The stopcocks for the water should be made so they can be regulated: make two cones: one solid, one hollow, finished on the lathe so that one of them can fit inside the other, and their telescoping on the same bar should make it so that there is either a strong or a gentle flow of water into the tank. Thus, by these principles the outfitting of a clock for use in winter can be assembled using water.

Clocks like these became common, for example, in court proceedings, to grant a speaker an allotted time to make his argument, of which there are several sources including one in the only ancient Roman novel to survive in its entirety, The Golden Ass by Apuleius:

'THE CLERK *of the Court began bawling again, this time summoning the chief witness to appear. Up stepped an old man, whom I did not know. He was invited to speak for as long as there was water in the clock; this was a hollow globe into which water was poured through a funnel in the neck, and from which it gradually escaped through fine perforations at the base.*'

CLEPSYDRA OR WATER CLOCK, 300 B.C.

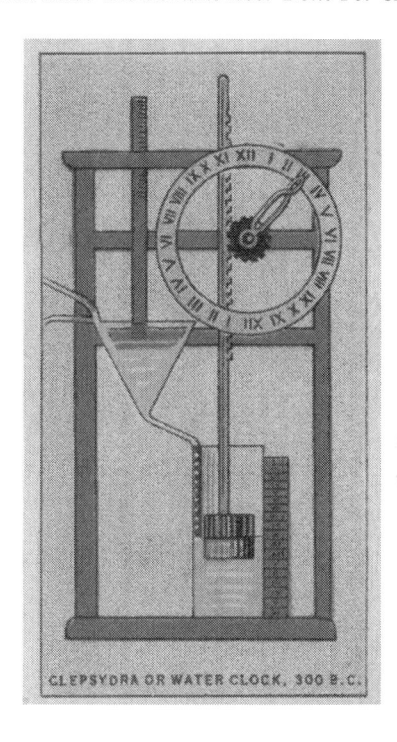

Roman water clocks became increasingly more complex over time. The image shows a water clock from around 300 BC. (Illustrator: Unknown)

And clock-makers all over the later western world believed that standard numerals would diminish the look of their great works of craftsmanship, so decided to give them a classier look by linking them with antiquity, resulting in a countless number of clock faces with Roman numerals, particularly famous public ones like the U.K.'s Big Ben, the Astronomical Clock in Prague or the Savior Tower in the Kremlin, Moscow, as well as countless others.

Just one more way that the Romans were ahead of their time.

24

TOWN PLANNING

Before the spread of the Roman Republic began around 500 BC, Europe consisted largely of scattered settlements rather than towns. Homes, for want of a better word, were largely made of wood, wattle and daub (manure/clay/hay) with straw thatching. These dwellings were usually scattered randomly about an area, with little or no thought given to alignment or organisation. The Romans changed all of that.

To be fair, Rome learned a great deal about town planning from the Greeks, but then as usual put their own imprint on the Grecian ideas. The Greek philosopher Hippodamus of Miletus is often considered the 'father of urban planning' and is credited with creating the concept of 'orthogonal town layout' or in other words, everything at right angles. That Romans initially adopted this is evident not from the towns that they built, but from their military machine.

A Roman army camp (*castrum*) was remarkably similar to what would later become towns and cities all over Europe. Their tents were organised in a strict grid pattern - they featured a *decumanus*, or east west main road that was wider than the other paths through the encampment, and a *cardo,* or north-south main road. These roads intersected at or near a central area, or *forum*, which housed the organisational structure. The roads also terminated in gates, through which supply lines were maintained and allowed for quick defence on all sides. The *castrum* was also fortified with a stockade, usually made of wood or earth, and a ditch. So well-planned were Roman military camps, that they became the basis of many Roman stone and concrete-built towns, and in fact, the emperor Augustus even gave one of his fortresses to the Astures tribe in Spain to be used as their capital.

The orthogonal pattern of streets and buildings is evident from this image of the Roman port of Ostia, which was based on a military camp or castrum. (Photo by Colin C. Murphy)

THE GREAT ROMAN ARCHITECT, Vitruvius, regarded urban planning as key to the successful organisational and visual impact of a city, and added considerably to the original Greek model, introducing elements such as sanitation, defence, the maximising of public convenience by the efficient locating of meeting areas and public facilities such as theatres, temples, markets and baths.

And Roman influence in urban planning extends well beyond Europe. Countless cities in the Middles Ages either simply evolved from the original Roman settlement or were newly constructed using the Roman model. These had a concentration of government and public facilities towards the centre, were located near or on a water source, like a river, often included a central open space for mass gatherings, and radiated out from there in a distinctive grid pattern. They usually also had a defensive wall and gates featuring a *portcullis* (gate that could be lowered) and a water-filled moat, reflecting the ditch surrounding the Roman castrum. The number of famous cities and towns actually founded by the Romans in Europe is immense, including Vienna and Salsburg in Austria, Paris and Lyon in France, Bonn, Cologne and Stuttgart in Germany, Rome (obviously!), Turin, Salerno and Bologna in Italy, Valencia, Pamplona and Seville in Spain, as well as Budapest (Hungary), London (UK), and Zurich (Switzerland) along with a myriad of others too innumerable to name. Many of the ideas that they introduced are still evident today, despite the modernization and redevelopment of these cities.

During the eighteenth and nineteenth centuries, architects and urban planners took many of these ideas with them when they moved to the colonies of Britain, France, Spain and so on, so that the Roman concepts of town planning ultimately spread to the Americas, Africa and the Far East, making it a truly global legacy. Even the word 'urban' comes from the Roman word for city - '*urbs*.'

So next time you're travelling around a well-planned city, remember that you'd most likely be lost without the Romans.

25

A VARIETY OF OTHER STUFF

The legacy of ancient Rome is so vast that it could easily fill a library in itself and the tentacles of their innovations, inventions and philosophies stretch across time into countless aspects of our lives, big and small. This is a mixed bag of some of the less obvious things that are Roman in origin but still a part of our lives today.

Rings as symbols of loyalty, friendship, eternity, the gods and so on have been around since the ancient Egyptians, usually made of fabric or leather. But it was the Romans who gave the world the metal wedding band. The ring was called the *anulus pronubus* and was not made of gold, but of iron, it being a symbol of the unbreakable bond between the couple. It was also a symbol of a transaction of sorts – in Roman society, an unmarried woman belonged to her father, but with her marriage, ownership was transferred to her new husband, and the ring was a symbol not only of their bond, but that the legal transfer had been made!

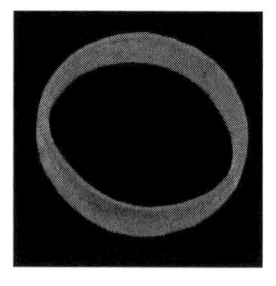

A typical Roman iron wedding ring.
(Photo by Colin C. Murphy)

∼

A RELATED TRADITION is one that virtually everyone, married or unmarried, is familiar with. You've seen it in a hundred movies, and you might have done it yourself, or had it done to you. When a groom lands back at the new home after tying the knot, assuming he doesn't have any serious back trouble, he lifts his new bride up and carries her across the threshold of the house into her new life. All very sweet and romantic.

The tradition's origins are actually quite dark and can be traced right back before the Roman Empire or even the Republic. In fact you'd have to go back to the legendary founder of Rome - Romulus himself.

A highly popular subject for Renaissance and post-Renaissance painters was the mythological incident known as 'The Rape of the Sabines' – there are at least eight paintings by different artists of the event. It's not quite as nasty as it sounds, however, as classical scholars used the word *'raptio'* to describe the event, which was mistranslated as 'rape', when in fact it more accurately refers to 'kidnapping'.

The story goes like this. Romulus had just founded Rome in 753 BC and a year later he realised that his near-exclusively male band of followers would require some women with whom to procreate if their new city was to thrive through the ages. The Sabines were a race of people inhabiting a large area north of Rome. So Romulus decided to invite them and multiple other tribes to a lavish festival in honour of an ancient god. With the party in full swing and the wine flowing, Romulus gave a signal and his Roman comrades seized the Sabine women and carried them off to their city. Romulus reputedly promised the women civic and property rights if they would accept their fate and marry the Roman men, and apparently they eventually acquiesced.

The Rape of the Sabine Women by Sebastiano Ricci (1700), which according to the Roman author Plutarch, was the origin of 'carrying over the threshold'. (Liechtenstein Museum, Vienna)

The action naturally upset all the other tribes, not least the Sabines. The tribes attacked Roman territory one after the other and Romulus defeated each in turn. Then the Sabines came looking for revenge – and their womenfolk back. The legend goes that in the midst of the violent battle, the Sabine women ran out of the city and hurled themselves between their fathers and their new Roman husbands begging them to stop killing each other. According to the Roman historian, Livy, they proclaimed that *'It was better that we perish than live widowed or fatherless without one or other of you!'*

The warring tribes ceased their conflict, the Sabines embraced the Romans and agreed to unite in a single kingdom, their combined strength giving them the first foothold that allowed them to expand their domain far and wide, and saw the beginnings of what was to become Roman domination of almost the entire European continent and beyond. So it's sort of a happy ending, especially if you're Roman.

The Romans carrying the women away and it ultimately resulting in the uniting of two tribes came be symbolised in marriage – the groom carrying the bride over the threshold was a symbol of different families uniting as one greater, stronger family. Which is probably hard to take for anyone nowadays who simply can't stand his or her in-laws.

~

WHEN THE NEWLYWEDS arrived at their new home they would probably prefer it to be nice and cosy. So it's just as well the Romans also gave the world central heating in the form of the *hypocaust*. Unfortunately this was limited to the wealthier citizens with large homes, yet it was impressive for its time.

The hypocaust consisted of a raised floor (about half a metre), supported by columns of stone or tiles set an arm's length apart, allowing air to circulate freely around them. A furnace, usually in an adjoining room, supplied continuous heat that was blown around the columns using a slave-operated bellows, heating the floors of the rooms above. Flues set into the walls could carry the heat to the upper floor and also allowed the hot air to escape through vents. Hypocausts were popular all over the Romans' domains, but particularly well appreciated in Northern Europe, in places like Gaul, Germany and Britain, and it's easy to understand why!

The hypocaust (centre) below what was once the floor of the Chesters Roman Fort, at Hadrian's Wall, England. (Photo by Steven Fruitsmaak)

∽

FOR ROMAN CITIZENS at the other end of the financial scale, life could be tough, and just getting enough food to avoid starvation was occasionally a factor in their lives, depending on whether the state was at war or if a person was unable to work through injury or illness, or if the grain harvest had been poor and so on.

The Lex Frumentaria *and later the* Cura Annonae *ensured a ready supply of grain for the poor. (Fresco from the House of Julia Felix, Pompeii. Museo Archeologico Nazionale, Naples.)*

Situations like this could cause unrest so various laws were introduced in the first century BC to lessen the likelihood of poor people starving, which in effect was the world's first state-subsidised welfare system.

The *Lex Frumentaria* (Corn laws) ensured that grain was sold to poorer citizens at a much lower price.

Matters improved further under Emperor Augustus with the *Cura Annonae,* (Care for the grain supply). The government provided a dole of subsidized or free grain, and later bread, to about a quarter of a million poorer citizens.

Emperor Trajan introduced another important act with the *Alimenta* (nourishment) - a welfare program that helped orphans and poor children throughout Italy, providing general funds, as well as food and subsidized education.

A VERY MINOR ROMAN LEGACY, but one that will be familiar to anyone who works with print, design or advertising, is the famous *'Lorem ipsum dolor...'* passage that is used as temporary filler while the actual text is being written. What most people don't know is that it is taken directly from Cicero's work *'De Finibus Bonorum et Malorum'* (On the Ends of Good and Evil) which is a philosophical tome in the form of dialogues recounted by Cicero to his friend Brutus. If only poor Cicero was alive to witness the daily misuse of his great work in trivial little ads and on the labels of tins of spaghetti hoops!

That's one to bore your colleagues with next time you encounter *'Lorem ipsum dolor...'*

An old cigarette advert with the Lorem Ipsum text highlighted where the actual text will be placed.

THE ROMANS also originated a great number of medical instruments, some of which wouldn't look out of place in a modern hospital, and others that might make you cringe, or look like something you might use to change a tractor tyre.

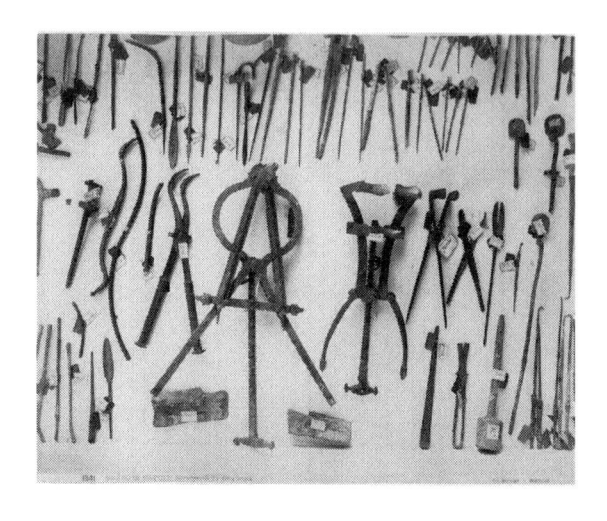

*A collection of scary-looking ancient
Roman medical implements.
(Photo by Giorgio Sommer.
Museo Archeologico Nazionale, Naples.)*

These included scalpels, surgical scissors, forceps, a rectal or vaginal speculum, bone drills, trepanning drills for brain surgery, S-shaped metal male catheters and a straighter one for women, and surgical saws, along with a whole lot more too wince-inducing to describe.

INSTRUMENTS such as these might have borne the name of their creator, as the Romans gave the world trademarks and logos. Marks upon goods were common among the Romans and from Syria to Britain are found the names of workmen, manufacturers and traders, along with pictorial identifications and marks of origin. Everything from chiselled stone blocks to wine amphorae to oil lamps bore a trademark of some sort, demonstrating an evident pride in the maker's work.

Several small amphorae (earthenware jars) found in Pompeii bear the stamp *'Lotion of Gavia Severa'* a local maker of supposedly medicinal potions. Two miniature glass bottles that once contained mercury and that were dated from the second century are stamped with the letters SCV - likely the glassmaker's initials. A bowl from Gaul made about 70 AD is marked inside with the inscription *'OF CEN'*: OF for Officina, or workshop, and CEN, which was most likely the name 'Censorinus.'

A Roman lead water pipe unearthed in Ravenna clearly bearing the trademark of its maker.
(Photo by José Luis. Museo Nazionale di Ravenna)

Even some slaves had a sort of trademark of ownership! A

bronze collar is inscribed with the instruction to bring back the slave in case of escape from his fifth century master, Scholasticus. It reads *'Hold me, lest I flee!'* along with an address where the fugitive could be returned for a reward.

∼

AND THE SUBJECT of trademarks is a fitting place for us to end, for it seems that an enormous amount of our modern world, in terms of language, culture, art, architecture, trade, infrastructure and engineering could quite easily be stamped with a single trademark denoting its origin – SPQR.

*SPQR – The Senate and People of Rome.
Inscribed on a statue in
The Piazza Campidoglio, Rome.
(Photo by Colin C. Murphy)*

FREE BOOK!

If you liked 'What Have The Romans Ever Done For Us?', you'll absolutely adore 'The Lost Voices Trilogy'. And you can get a free copy of 'The Lost Voices - Prelude' by visiting my website at colincharlesmurphy.com

The Lost Voices is an epic trilogy of ancient Pompeii based around the thousands of fascinating graffiti that the inhabitants scratched on the town's walls. Often touching, earthy, humorous

or philosophical, these small scratchings give us wonderful personal insights into the lives of real Pompeians. Here is a small sample:

- *Our beautiful daughter was born early on Saturday, August 2.*
- *Here slept Vibius Restitutus alone, his heart filled with longings for his Urbana.*
- *My lusty son, with how many girls have you f...ed?*
- *Saturninus lived just 1 year, 7 months*
- *Marcus says a big hello to his mother Cossinia.*
- *Actius, master of the stage performers!*
- *Celadus the Thracian gladiator makes the girls moan!*

Read the electrifying introduction to this highly original trilogy in 'The Lost Voices - Prelude'. It is the amazing story of ancient Pompeii brought to life in the words of Pompeians themselves. The story will capture your imagination and hold it prisoner until the final word!

To get your free copy of
'The Lost Voices - Prelude' visit
colincharlesmurphy.com

ALSO BY COLIN C. MURPHY

Visit Colin C. Murphy's website at **colincharlesmurphy.com** where you can discover more of his critically acclaimed books including:

The Lost Voices Trilogy

'3 beautifully crafted historical novels...I was totally immersed...lots of twists and turns...a great read!'

- Amazon reviews

'Five stars. A superb and gripping story set against one of the most devastating events in history.'

- Amazon reviews

More over page...

Boycott

'A hugely ambitious debut novel... minute research and well-drawn characters...a valuable piece of writing...unforgettably harrowing... deserves a wide readership.' - *Irish Independent Literary Supplement*

'Masterful storytelling... perfectly paced and beautifully written. Its achievement is impressive.' - *Frank McGuinness, playwright, author, poet, winner of New York Drama Critics award and Bafta nominee.*

'A rattling yarn, with action racing along, brilliant twists, flawed heroes and evil villains...a stirring and deeply researched story.' - *Books Ireland*

'A brilliantly written and moving work of fiction. Deserves five stars, as for its genre, it really is that good. - *Goodreads.com*

The Priest Hunters

'There is a crying need for a more novelistic approach to tell the stories of the past, one which brings history alive. And this Murphy has done in a compelling, gripping and often disturbing book.'

- *Irish Independent*

'A compelling account of a time period in Irish history.'

- *Goodreads.*

'An incredible account of some of the most hated men in Ireland.'
- *Amazon.*

'A fascinating book.'

- *Amazon*

Fierce History

'Murphy recounts 5,000 years of little-known tales from around the world exploring historical figures on the fringes whose exploits will both intrigue and revolt readers!'

- Daily Mirror

Colin Murphy welcomes you to the fringes of history where shocking tales and compelling facts await you.

- Waterford Observer

'Five Stars'

- Goodreads.

PLEASE LEAVE A REVIEW

If you have enjoyed this book, I would really appreciate it if you would leave a brief review.
Independent authors or those with small publishers simply do not have the resources to compete with the big publishing houses in terms of advertising or influencing reviewers in the press and other media. So we rely on you, dear reader, to help balance the scales a little.

Reviews help authors enormously in
bringing their work to a wider audience.

To leave a review simply visit your online
point of purchase and scroll down to
'Customer Reviews'.
Thank you!

Copyright © 2020 by Cygnia Publishing/Colin C. Murphy

No part of this publication may be reproduced, distributed, or transmitted in any form or by any means, including photocopying, recording, or other electronic or mechanical methods, without the prior written permission of the publisher, except in the case of brief quotations embodied in critical reviews and certain other non-commercial uses permitted by copyright law.

What Have The Romans Ever Done For Us?
Text copyright © Colin C. Murphy, 2020
Cover design © Donal O'Dea, 2020

All rights reserved.

The right of Colin C. Murphy to be identified as the author of this work has been asserted by him in accordance with the Copyright & Related Rights Act, 2000.

© Colin C. Murphy 2020

BIBLIOGRAPHY

Advertising

- Advertising among the Romans by Evan T. Sage
- The Classical Weekly, Vol. 9, No. 26 (May 6, 1916), pp. 202-208
- Published by: The Johns Hopkins University Press.
- https://ancient-rome.info/ - Ancient Roman advertisements.
- www.kapokmarketing.com - Marketing Is Not New; Lessons from the Ancient Roman City of Pompeii.
- The Encyclopaedia of Ephemera: A Guide to the Fragmentary Documents of Everyday Life by Maurice Rickards

Agriculture

- The Efficiency of Roman Farming under the Empire by Kenneth D. White
- Agricultural History, Vol. 30, No. 2 (Apr., 1956), pp. 85-89.

- http://factsanddetails.com - Agriculture in ancient Rome.
- The Archaeology of the Roman Economy by K. Greene, pp. 67-94. 1986 by the University of California Press.
- https://erenow.net - Agriculture, Roman.
- https://www.academia.edu - Roman Agriculture and Food Production.

Alphabet

- 'The stories behind the letters of our alphabet' by Susannah Cahalan. The New York Post, February 8, 2015.
- www.superprof.co.uk - The Origin of Latin Letters.
- The Shape of Script. How and why writing systems change. Edited by Stephen D. Houston.
- https://en.wikipedia.org/wiki/Latin_alphabet
- The Etruscan Origin of the Roman Alphabet and the Names of the Letters by B. L. Ullman. Classical Philology, Vol. 22, No. 4 (Oct., 1927), pp. 372-377.

Aqueducts

- The Building of the Roman Aqueducts by Esther Boise Van Deman. McGrath Publishing Company, 1934.
- www.nationalgeographic.org - Roman Aqueducts.
- www.nationalgeographic.org - Aqueducts: Quenching Rome's Thirst.
- www.unrv.com - Ancient Roman Aqueducts.
- https://www.ancient.eu/aqueduct/

Architecture

- http://www.ancient.eu/Roman_Architecture/
- https://en.wikipedia.org/wiki/Ancient_Roman_architecture
- https://beebreeders.com - How Roman architecture influenced modern architecture
- https://interestingengineering.com/ - 21 Famous Buildings and Monuments Influenced by Roman Architecture
- https://www.forbes.com - The Physics Of Ancient Roman Architecture by Chad Orzel. July 5, 2016.
- City: A Story of Roman Planning and Construction by David McCaulay. October 1983.

Birthday Cake

- Tristia by Ovid. Tristia III, XIII. A Birthday at Tomis.
- https://en.wikipedia.org/wiki/Birthday_cake
- https://www.irishtimes.com - The Sweet History of Birthday Cakes by Aoife McElwain. July 17, 2016.
- https://www.huffpost.com - This Is Why You Get To Celebrate Your Birthday Every Year by Todd Van Luling. November 11, 2013.

Bound Books

- http://www.ancientpages.com - Ancient Romans Invented The First Bound Book.
- https://en.wikipedia.org/wiki/Codex
- https://www.thebalancecareers.com - Codex, the Earliest Form of a Bound Book by Valerie Peterson. December 16, 2018.

- https://www.history.com - 10 Innovations That Built Ancient Rome.
- http://www.bbc.com - The mysterious ancient origins of the book by Keith Houston. August 22, 2016.

Bureaucracy

- https://web.ics.purdue.edu - Civic Life in the Roman Empire under the Aelians.
- Imperial Bureaucrats in the Roman Provinces by Ramsay MacMullen. Harvard Studies in Classical Philology, Vol. 68 (1964), pp. 305-316
- https://en.wikipedia.org/wiki/Bureaucracy
- https://www.cambridge.org - 'The Late Roman Empire Was before All Things a Bureaucratic State' by Michael Whitby. University of Birmingham, published by Cambridge University Press.
- http://factsanddetails.com - Bureaucracy and Administration in the Roman Empire.

Calendar

- https://www.forbes.com - The History of the Birthday And The Roman Calendar by Sarah Bond. October 1, 2016.
- https://www.britannica.com - The early Roman calendar.
- https://en.wikipedia.org/wiki/Roman_calendar
- https://www.livescience.com - Keeping Time: Months and the Modern Calendar by Robert Coolman. May 16, 2014.
- 'What did the Romans do for a calendar before Julius Caesar?' By Roger Schlueter.

Christmas/Saturnalia

- Belleville News-Democrat, March 27, 2018.

- https://www.historytoday.com - 'Did the Romans invent Christmas?' by Matt Salusbury. December 12, 2009.
- https://www.history.com - Saturnalia. 'Is Christmas a pagan holiday? August 21, 2018.
- https://www.britannica.com - Saturnalia, Roman Festival.
- https://www.ancient.eu/Saturnalia/
- https://www.ancient-origins.net - Saturnalia: The December Festival of Joy and Merriment in Ancient Rome

Concrete

- https://www.sciencemag.org - 'Why modern mortar crumbles, but Roman concrete lasts millennia.' By Zahra Ahmad. July 3, 2017.
- https://en.wikipedia.org/wiki/Roman_concrete
- http://www.engineersjournal.iev-vv - Do as the Romans did: how natural chemistry strengthened ancient concrete. July 18, 2017.
- https://www.theguardian.com - 'Why Roman concrete still stands strong while modern version decays' by Nicola Davis. July 4, 2017
- https://www.nature.com - 'Seawater is the secret to long-lasting Roman concrete.' By Alexandra Witze. July 3, 2017.

Fast Food

- https://www.businessinsider.com - 'Fast food has existed since ancient Rome' by Áine Cain. June 13, 2019.
- https://www.smithsonianmag.com - 'Recently Uncovered Thermopolium Reminds Us That Romans Loved Fast Food as Much as We Do' by Jason Daley. April 3, 2019.
- http://www.ancientpages.com - 'Thermopolium – Ancient Roman Restaurant Offered Fast Food But Was It A Good Idea To Eat There?' by Ellen Lloyd. April 5, 2019.
- https://www.theguardian.com - 'Pompeii 'fast food' bar unearthed in ancient city after 2,000 years' by Angela Giuffrida. March 27, 2019.

Government

- https://www.ancient.eu/Roman_Government/
- The afterlife of the Roman Senate by Catherine Steel. January 3, 2016. Oxford University Press
- https://www.ancientfacts.net - 'What was ancient Rome's influence on government and democracy today?'
- https://www.britannica.com - The Roman Republic.
- https://www.smithsonianmag.com -
- 'Lessons in the Decline of Democracy From the Ruined Roman Republic' by Jason Daley. November 6, 2018.

Guide Dogs

- https://www.guidedogs.org.uk - The History of Guide Dogs.

- 'Dogs' Miscellany: Everything You Always Wanted to Know About Man's Best Friend' by J. A. Wines. Published by Michael O'Mara, 2013
- https://www.igdf.org.uk - International Guide Dog Federation – The History of Guide Dogs.

International Currency

- http://numismatics.org - Rome: A Thousand Years of Monetary History.
- https://www.coinbooks.org - JUNO Moneta, Goddess of Money.
- https://www.armstrongeconomics.com - 'The Monetary History of the Roman Republic' by Martin A. Armstrong.
- https://en.wikipedia.org/wiki/Roman_currency

Language & Phrases

- https://www.nationalgeographic.org - Traces of Ancient Rome in the Modern World. July 6, 2018.
- https://www.historytoday.com - The Language of the Roman Empire.
- https://en.wikipedia.org/wiki/Legacy_of_the_Roman_Empire
- https://www.worldhistory.biz - The Legacy of Rome.
- https://www.babbel.com - 'Latinus Pro Stultis — 15 Latin Phrases We Still Use Today' by Cristina Gusano. May 23, 2017.
- https://www.inklyo.com - '24 Latin Phrases You Use Every Day (And What They Mean)' by Erica Urie. October 7, 2015.

Mail Service

- https://www.smithsonianmag.com - 'Scholars Translate Ancient Guilt Trip in Letter From Soldier to Family' by Mary Beth Griggs. Match 27, 2014.
- https://www.britannica.com/topic/cursus-publicus
- https://bathpostalmuseum.org.uk/ - 500 BC: The Roman Postal System.
- https://qns.com/ - 'Sophisticated postal service existed in ancient Rome' by Joan Brown Wettingfeld. July 20, 2012.
- https://www.csun.edu - Letter of Apion.
- Travel & Geography in the Roma Empire, Ed. Colin Adams and Ray Laurence, p. 2001.
- The speed of the Roman Imperial Post by A.M.Ramsey. Journal of Roman Studies 15, 1925, 60-74.

Military Strategy

- https://www.bartleby.com - Greek and Roman Military Influences in Modern Warfare. February 21, 2018.
- https://www.romanarmytalk.com - Roman Army Influence on Modern Warfare
- https://en.wikipedia.org/wiki/Strategy_of_the_Roman_military
- https://historum.com - How influential and revolutionary is Roman warfare?
- https://www.mountvernon.org - Fabian Strategy by Gregory J. Dehler, Front Range Community College.
- Polybius, Livy and the 'Fabian Strategy' by Paul Erdkamp. Ancient Society, Vol. 23 (1992), pp. 127-147.

Political Campaigning

- Pompeii: A Sourcebook - By Alison E. Cooley, M. G. L. Cooley
- https://members.classicalconversations.com - 'How to Campaign and Win a Roman Election—How the Romans Were Just Like Us!' by Kathy Sheppard. November 2, 2012.
- Political Campaigns in Roman Municipalities by Eva Matthews Sanford
- The Classical Journal, Vol. 25, No. 6 (Mar., 1930.
- https://www.italymagazine.com - 'Ancient Graffiti At Pompeii: Early Wall Posts And Political Slogans' by Carol King. February 2, 1023.
- https://www.ancient.eu - Pompeii: Graffiti, Signs & Electoral Notices.

Roads

- https://www.acorn-ind.co.uk - The Influence of Roman Engineering on the Contemporary World.
- https://www.ancient.eu - Roman Tunnels.
- https://www.dailymail.co.uk - 'How the Romans shaped today's economy: Roads paved 2,000 years ago STILL contribute to the spread of wealth, satellite images reveal' by Joe Pinkstone. April 30, 2018.
- https://www.atlasobscura.com/ - 'The Beautiful Network of Ancient Roman Roads' by Chris White. June 19, 2015.
- https://www.ancient-origins.net - 'Built to Last: The Secret that Enabled Roman Roads to Withstand the Passage of Time.' February 10, 2017. DHWTY.

Sanitation

- https://www.therthdimension.org - Sanitation during the late Roman Republic.
- https://www.medicaldaily.com - 'Ancient Roman Bathhouses Were Actually Very Unclean, Spread Around Intestinal Parasites' by Steve Smith. January 7, 2016.
- http://easteuropeanstudies.blogspot.com - How has ancient Roman technology affected modern life?
- https://www.explore-italian-culture.com - Ancient Roman Baths: how they helped Italy become one of the healthiest cultures in Europe.
- https://phys.org - What toilets and sewers tells us about ancient Roman sanitation.
- https://en.wikipedia.org/wiki/Sanitation_in_ancient_Rome

Timekeeping

- Daily Life in the Roman City: Rome, Pompeii and Ostia by Gregory S. Aldrete. U. of Oklahoma Press, 2008.
- https://en.wikipedia.org/wiki/Roman_timekeeping
- https://www.thehourglass.com - 'Timekeeping in the Roman Army' by Professor George Cupcea. July 7, 2018.
- https://nomenclatorbooks.com - Roman timekeeping.
- 'The Concept of Time in Ancient Rome' by Samuel L. Macey. International Social Science Review. Vol. 65, No. 2 (Spring 1990).

Town Planning

- https://www.academia.edu - Analyse how the Greeks and Romans influenced the planning development and management of western and non-western cities.'
- The Influence of Roman Military Camps on Town Planning' by Robert Lyon
- State University of New York at Potsdam.
- https://en.wikipedia.org/wiki/History_of_urban_planning
- https://www.academia.edu/ - The main principles of Roman town planning.

A Variety of Other Stuff

Wedding rings

- https://www.ancient-origins.net - Roman Engagement and Wedding Rings: Joining Hands and Hearts. March 3, 2017.
- https://www.claddaghdesign.com - The History of the Wedding Ring.
- https://www.vanityfair.com/ - Band For Life: The History of Wedding Rings
- https://en.wikipedia.org/wiki/Engagement_ring

Carrying over threshold

- https://www.pbs.org - Weddings, Marriage & Divorce.
- Marriage Customs of the World: An Encyclopaedia of Dating Customs, Volume 1
- By George P. Monger
- https://www.ancient-origins.net - The Rape of the Sabine Women. February 2, 2015.

Hypocaust

- https://www.britannica.com/technology/hypocaust
- https://www.romanobritain.org/ - Roman Central Heating.
- http://www.ancientpages.com - First Central Heating Invented By Ancient Romans 2,000 Years Ago.

Welfare

- A Dictionary of Greek and Roman Antiquities, by John Murray, 1875.
- https://fee.org - Poor Relief in Ancient Rome' by Henry Hazlitt. April 1, 1971.
- The Origins of Roman Experiments in Social Welfare by Frank C. Bourne
- The Classical Weekly, Vol. 44, No. 3 (Dec. 4, 1950).

Lorem ipsum

- https://en.wikipedia.org/wiki/Lorem_ipsum
- https://priceonomics.com - The History of Lorem ipsum.

Surgical Implements

- https://www.romanobritain.org - On Roman Surgery.
- http://exhibits.hsl.virginia.edu/ - A Display of Surgical Instruments from Antiquity
- https://www.medicalnewstoday.com - Ancient Roman Medicine: Influences, practice and learning.

Trademarks

- 'Some Historical Matter concerning Trade-Marks' by Edward S. Rogers. Michigan Law Review, Vol. 9, No. 1 (Nov., 1910).
- https://www.english-heritage.org.uk - Seven ingenious things the Romans brought to Britain.
- 'Exhibit explores ancient Roman 'designer' labels, trademarks' by Frances D'Emilio, Associated Press. June 16, 2016. San Diego Union-Tribune.

ACKNOWLEDGMENTS

My thanks to Donal O'Dea for the cover design, which is up to his usual high standards. My gratitude also to the people who snapped many of the images and posted them into the public domain on Wikimedia Commons:
Post du Gard photo by Patrick Clenet.
Plăcintă cake photo by Nicubunu.
Pompeii stone inscription photo by René Voorburg.
La jeunesse de Bacchus photo by leo.jeje.
Lead pipe trademark photo by José Luis.
Museo Nazionale di Ravenna

Licences: https://creativecommons.org/licenses/by-sa/4.0/deed.en

ABOUT THE AUTHOR

Colin C. Murphy is the author of the critically acclaimed historical novel Boycott, The Lost Voices trilogy set in ancient Pompeii, and has also penned numerous historical non-fiction books. Formerly a multi-award winning creative director of an advertising agency, he quit the business a decade ago for his first professional love, writing. He has had a fascination with the ancient Roman world since childhood, and has researched extensively in Rome, Pompeii, Ostia Antica, El-Jem in Tunisia, Arles in France and Italica in Spain. He also has a love of history in general, and is particularly interested in exploring the lives and stories of the past's lesser known, yet no less fascinating, men and women. When not writing or travelling he enjoys hill-walking, and has climbed every mountain in Ireland. He lives in Dublin with his family.